UK Ninja Dual Zone Air Fryer Cookbook 2023

1600 Days Easy and Budget-Friendly Recipes You Will Love incl. Dinners, Sides, Snacks, Lunches & More (European Measurements & UK Ingredients)

Doris B. Hughes

Contents

CHAPTER 7 SNACKS & APPETIZERS

CHAPTER 8 HEALTHY VEGETARIAN & VEGAN RECIPES 71

How to Use the Ninja Foodi Dual Zone Air Fryer: A Beginner's Guide

As a busy mom myself, with a 9-to-5 job, I understand the struggle of finding time to cook healthy meals for my family. Between work, kids, and household chores, there just never seems to be enough time in the day. However, being a busy mom doesn't have to mean sacrificing healthy meals for your family. By implementing strategies like meal planning, choosing the right kitchen appliance and giving yourself grace, you can still provide your family with nutritious meals while juggling all of life's demands.

I have always been fascinated with the idea of cooking with an air fryer. I had heard so many good things about it from my friends and family, and I was eager to try it out for myself. Finally, after months of contemplating, I decided to purchase the Ninja Dual Zone Air Fryer and experiment with it in my kitchen. At first, I was a little intimidated by the air fryer. It was bigger than I had anticipated, and it had so many buttons and features that I didn't know where to begin. But after reading through the instruction manual, I decided to start small and make some French fries. I cut up some potatoes, drizzled them with oil, and then placed them in my Ninja Dual Zone Air Fryer. I set the temperature and the timer and waited anxiously for the fries to cook! As the timer counted down, I could hear the air fryer humming and sizzling away. When the timer finally beeped, I opened the unit to reveal perfectly crispy and golden-brown fries! They were hot and delicious, and I couldn't believe that they had been cooked with just a fraction of the oil that I wouldn't normally use.

Over the next few weeks, I experimented with different recipes and ingredients in my Ninja Dual Zone Air Fryer. I made everything from chicken wings to roasted vegetables, and each dish turned out better than the last. I was amazed at how quickly and easily the Ninja Dual Zone Air Fryer cooked my food, and I loved the fact that it was so much healthier than other cooking methods. One of my favourite things to make in the Ninja Dual Zone Air Fryer was chicken nuggets. I would dip the chicken pieces in a mixture of flour and spices, then spray it with cooking spray and place it in the Ninja Dual Zone Air Fryer. In just a few minutes, the chicken nuggets would come out perfectly crispy on the outside and tender on the inside. It was a healthier and more delicious alternative to deep-fried nuggets! As I continued to use my Ninja Dual Zone Air Fryer, I began to appreciate its versatility and convenience. I could cook a wide variety of dishes in it, and it was much faster than using an oven or stovetop. Plus, it was so easy to clean – all I had to do was wipe it down with a damp cloth. To sum up, I was so happy with my decision to purchase the Ninja Dual Zone Air Fryer. It had quickly become one of my favourite kitchen appliances, and I couldn't imagine cooking without it. I loved experimenting with new recipes and creating healthy, delicious meals for myself and my family! And so this book came to be!

Getting to Know your Ninja Foodi Dual Zone

The Ninja Dual Zone Air Fryer is a kitchen appliance that allows you to cook a wide variety of foods with little to no oil, making it a healthier option than traditional frying methods. It features two separate cooking zones, each with its temperature and timer controls, allowing you to cook multiple foods at once with different settings. My Ninja Dual Zone Air Fryer has a 3.8-litre capacity, which is a great option for individuals or small families. It can cook up to 2 pounds of

French fries or chicken wings in one go! The appliance also has six cooking functions, including air frying, air broiling, roasting, reheating, dehydrating, and baking. The air fry function is particularly popular, as it can cook food to a crispy texture without the need for excess oil. The Ninja Dual Zone Air Fryer also has a wide temperature range, from 40°C to 230°C, giving you the ability to cook a variety of dishes. One unique feature of the Ninja Dual Zone Air Fryer is its smart finish function, which automatically switches to a lower temperature when the cooking time is up to prevent overcooking and ensure that your food remains hot and crispy.

The Ninja Dual Zone Air Fryer comes with two ceramic-coated baskets, which are non-stick and dishwasher safe. They are also free from harmful chemicals like PFOA and PTFE. The Ninja Dual Zone Air Fryer also has a digital control panel that makes it easy to set the temperature and cooking time, which can be adjusted to suit the type of food you are cooking. The control panel is user-friendly and easy to navigate. It features intuitive controls that make it easy to program and adjust cooking settings. Now, we come to the question – why do you need the Ninja Dual Zone Air Fryer?

First and foremost, air frying is a healthier alternative to traditional deep frying as it uses hot air circulation to cook food, resulting in crispy and tasty foods without the need for oil or grease. The Ninja Dual Zone Air Fryer uses 75% less fat than traditional frying methods, making it a healthier alternative! If you want to take your cooking up a notch, the Ninja Dual Zone Air Fryer may help you! With its customizable settings, the Ninja Dual Zone Air Fryer allows you to customize cooking settings according to your preferences, with options for temperature, time, and cooking modes. As a great time-saving solution, the dual-zone feature allows you to cook two different

foods at the same time with different cooking times and temperatures, making it easier to prepare complete meals. In a fraction of time! Further, let's consider its versatility! The Ninja Dual Zone Air Fryer can be used to air fry, roast, reheat, and dehydrate, making it a versatile kitchen appliance that can replace several other kitchen gadgets. The appliance is also compact and lightweight, making it easy to store in a small kitchen or pantry, taking up minimal counter space. It will save you a lot of money and kitchen space! The air fryer cooks food quickly and evenly, which can save time and energy in the kitchen. It uses less energy than a conventional oven, making it a more energy-efficient cooking option!

To sum up, the Ninja Dual Zone Air Fryer is a versatile and convenient appliance for anyone looking to cook healthier meals at home. Its dual zone design and multiple cooking functions make it a great option for preparing a variety of dishes, while its compact size makes it easy to store and use in any kitchen.

6 Features That Will Make You Want to Get the Ninja Foodi Dual Zone

The Ninja Air Fryer is a popular choice among home cooks and has received positive reviews for its performance, versatility, and multi-functionality. Let's look at the main features of the Ninja Dual Zone Air Fryer. The main unit is the central part of the air fryer that houses the heating elements, controls, and other internal components. The Ninja Dual Zone Air Fryer comes with two cooking baskets, allowing you to cook two different dishes at once. The baskets have a nonstick coating and a handle for easy removal. The capacity of both drawers and baskets is also impressive! There is enough room for a complete family meal! There are two crisper plates that you can use in place of the cooking baskets. The plates are designed to provide a crispy texture to your food, similar to deep-frying! Further, the drip tray collects any excess oil or grease that drips from the food during cooking. It's removable and dishwasher-safe. As an electric device, the Ninja Dual Zone Air has a power cord that you can use to plug into an electrical outlet. And last but not least, it comes with an instruction manual that provides detailed instructions on how to use the machine and its various features. It's important to note that these are the standard parts that come with the Ninja Dual Zone Air Fryer, but some models or packages may include additional accessories or attachments.

Air Frying – One of the key features of the Ninja Air Fryer is its ability to cook food with 75% less fat than traditional frying methods. This is achieved by using hot air and a fan to circulate it around the food, which creates a crispy outer layer without the need for oil. This makes it a healthier alternative to traditional frying methods, which can be high in calories and fat.

Roasting – The Ninja Air Fryer is not just limited to frying food. It can also be used to roast meat and vegetables, which gives them a crispy outer layer while keeping the inside moist and tender. For instance, it will take you about 40 minutes to roast whole beets; but, if you cook small chunks of peeled beets, it will take about 15 minutes. Wow!

Baking – One of the standout features of the Ninja Dual Zone Air Fryer is its ability to bake food. Any food, from casseroles to cakes, that can be cooked in a conventional oven can be prepared in the Ninja Dual Zone Air Fryer!

Air Broiling – My Ninja Dual Zone Air Fryer represents a union of high-tech kitchen tools and restaurant-style cooking techniques! It uses superheated air to broil your food to perfection.

Reheating – The appliance can also be used to reheat food, which helps to retain the original texture and flavour. You can also use up leftovers and minimize food vast! Win-win!

Dehydrating – Your Ninja Dual Zone Air Fryer comes with a dehydrating function that allows you to dry out fruits, vegetables, and meat for snacks like fruit chips or beef jerky. For the best results, slice the food thinly and arrange it in a single layer on the tray or basket of the air fryer. Set the temperature to the lowest setting and let the food dehydrate according to the manufacturer's instructions, checking it periodically to ensure that it's drying evenly.

How to Clean the Ninja Foodi Dual Zone Air Fryer?

Cleaning the Ninja Dual Zone Air Fryer is important to keep it in good condition, and working efficiently and hygienically. Regular cleaning is also essential to prevent any food residue buildup, which can affect the taste of your food and even cause health problems! Here's a step-by-step guide to help you clean your Ninja Dual Zone Air Fryer:

- First and foremost, unplug the unit and let it cool completely before cleaning.
- Remove the cooking basket and any accessories from the Ninja Dual Zone Air Fryer.
- Wipe the exterior of the air fryer with a damp cloth or a non-abrasive sponge. Never submerge heating elements in the water!
- Remove any food residue from the cooking basket and accessories with a soft-bristled brush or a non-abrasive sponge.
- Wash the cooking basket and accessories in warm, soapy water. You can also put cooking baskets and crisper plates in the dishwasher since they are dishwasher-safe. I recommend hand washing them to extend

the life of the air fryer accessories.

- Wipe the inside of the air fryer with a damp cloth. Be careful not to damage the heating elements or the non-stick coating. A soft-bristled brush also works well. Do not use abrasive cleaners or scouring pads as they can damage the non-stick coating!
- If there is stubborn food residue or grease buildup, you can use a non-abrasive cleaner or degreaser specifically designed for air fryers. Follow the manufacturer's instructions and rinse the air fryer thoroughly with clean water afterwards.
- For tough stains, mix baking soda and water to form a paste and use it to scrub the basket and pan.
- Dry the cooking basket, accessories, and the interior of the air fryer with a clean towel or let them air dry completely.
- Reassemble the air fryer and plug it back in.

Note: Always refer to the user manual for specific cleaning instructions and warnings.

What Are the Possible Risks of the Ninja Dual Zone?

However, like any cooking appliance, there are some risks associated with using the Ninja Dual Zone Air Fryer. Here are some potential risks to consider:

- The hot air produced by the air fryer can cause burns if you come into contact with it. It's important to use caution when handling the appliance, particularly the basket or tray, as they can become extremely hot.
- Air fryers use high temperatures and a lot of electricity to function, which can lead to the risk of fire if not used properly. It's important to follow the manufacturer's instructions carefully, avoid overcrowding the appliance, and never leave it unattended

while in use.

- While air fryers can be a healthier alternative to deep frying, there are still concerns about the potential health risks of consuming a lot of fried food. It's important to balance your diet and consume fried foods in moderation.
- Some air fryer baskets have a non-stick coating that can wear off over time and potentially contaminate your food. It's important to inspect the basket regularly and replace it if the coating starts to wear off.
- Air fryers are powered by electricity and may pose a risk of electrocution if they are not handled properly. It's important to always use the appliance in a dry environment and avoid using it if it appears damaged.

Air Fryer FAQs Tips and Tricks for the Ninja Dual Zone Air Fryer

What types of food can I cook in the Ninja Dual Zone Air Fryer?
You can cook a wide range of food, including chicken wings, French fries, fish, vegetables, and even desserts like doughnuts. You cannot cook watery foods such as soups and stews.

What type of oil should I use?
Use the right amount of oil: While air frying doesn't require as much oil as traditional frying, you'll still need to use some oil for the best results. Check the recipe for the recommended amount or use a small amount of oil spray to coat your food. Using cooking sprays can help prevent your food from sticking to the air fryer basket.

Is it necessary to shake the drawer?
Shaking the air fryer drawer during the cooking process can help ensure that your food is evenly cooked.

How much food can I cook in the Ninja Dual Zone Air Fryer?

The amount of food you can cook in the Ninja Dual Zone Air Fryer depends on the size of the appliance. Most models can accommodate up to 4-8 servings of food at a time.

Is it necessary to preheat my Ninja Dual Zone Air Fryer?

Preheating an air fryer is not always necessary, but it can help to ensure that the food cooks evenly and gets crispy on the outside. The amount of preheating time required will vary based on the model of the Ninja Dual Zone Air Fryer.

Can I use aluminium foil in my Ninja Dual Zone Air Fryer?

Yes, you can use aluminium foil, but it's important to avoid blocking the airflow or covering the entire basket with foil, as this can prevent the food from cooking evenly.

Is the Ninja Dual Zone Air Fryer safe to use?

Yes, air fryers are generally safe to use. However, it's important to follow the manufacturer's instructions. It's also important to keep it away from flammable materials and to not overcrowd the drawer with food. Plus, you will avoid the risks of defrosting your foods on the counter. The Ninja Dual Zone Air Fryer can cook frozen food to absolute perfection!

What will happen when overcrowding the basket?
Overcrowding the air fryer basket can lead to unevenly cooked food. Make sure to leave enough space between each item to allow for proper air circulation.

Whyte type of accessories can I use?

The Ninja Dual Zone Air Fryer comes with a variety of accessories, such as a crisper plate and a multi-layer rack. In general, you can use oven-safe pans and other bakeware. Experimenting with these accessories can help you prepare different types of food and achieve different textures.

Can I put frozen foods in my Ninja Dual Zone Air Fryer?

You do not need to defrost your food before cooking in the Ninja Dual Zone Air Fryer. Preheat the air fryer to the desired temperature according to the frozen food packaging instructions (or recipe). For example, if you're cooking frozen French fries, you may need to preheat the air fryer to 200°C.

Place the frozen food in the appropriate cooking zone. Make sure not to overcrowd the drawer so that the hot air can circulate the food. Set the cooking time and temperature according to the instructions on the frozen food packaging or your recipe. You can adjust the time and temperature depending on your desired level of crispiness. When the cooking cycle is complete, check the internal temperature of the food to ensure it has reached a safe temperature (this is particularly important for meat products). Remove the drawer from your Ninja Dual Zone Air Fryer and serve the cooked food immediately. Happy cooking!

Book Summary

The Ninja Foodi Dual Zone is a revolutionary air fryer that redefines healthy living. The Ninja Dual Zone Air Fryer is becoming increasingly popular in kitchens around the world. Whether you're making a delicious cake, roasting a chicken, or drying fruit, its user-friendliness and multi-functionality make it a great addition to any kitchen. With the Ninja Foodi Dual Zone, you can enjoy delicious meals with fewer calories and fat, while still enjoying all the flavours of your favourite foods. Whether you are a beginner or an experienced cook, the Ninja Dual Zone Air Fryer and this recipe collection will change your kitchen game forever! With 120 delicious, hand-picked recipes in which tradition and new technology come together, you won't run out of inspiration! Happy cooking!

CHAPTER 1 BREAKFAST

Mini Mushroom Frittatas

Serves 6

Prep time: 10 minutes / Cook time: 15 minutes

Ingredients
- 9 small eggs
- 100g cream cheese
- 1 small onion, chopped
- 150g brown mushrooms, chopped (or Italian cremini mushrooms)
- 1 tsp dried basil
- 1 tsp dried oregano
- 1 tsp dried Italian parsley (optional)
- Sea salt and ground black pepper, to taste

Preparation instructions
1. Remove a crisper plate from your Ninja Foodi. Brush silicone cases with nonstick oil.
2. Preheat the Ninja Foodi to 180°C for 5 minutes.
3. In a bowl, whisk the eggs until frothy; fold in the cream cheese and mix to combine well. Add the other Ingredients and whisk until everything is well incorporated.
4. Spoon the batter into the prepared silicone cases.
5. Select zone 1 and pair it with "BAKE" at 180°C for 15 minutes. Select "MATCH" followed by the "START/STOP" button.
6. Bon appétit!

Star Anise Muffins

Serves 8

Prep time: 10 minutes / Cook time: 15 minutes /

Ingredients
- 2 large eggs
- 300g apple sauce
- 200g brown sugar
- 100g coconut oil
- 200g self-raising plain flour
- A pinch of sea salt
- 1/4 tsp ground anise
- 1/4 tsp ground cinnamon

Preparation instructions
1. Remove a crisper plate from your Ninja Foodi. Preheat the Ninja Foodi to 160°C for 5 minutes. Spray 8 muffin cases with nonstick oil.
2. In a separate mixing bowl, whisk the eggs until pale and frothy. Slowly and gradually, stir in apple sauce, brown sugar, and coconut oil; mix until everything is well incorporated.
3. In another bowl, thoroughly combine the dry Ingredients.
4. Slowly and gradually, add the dry Ingredients to the wet Ingredients; mix again to combine. Spoon the batter into the prepared muffin cases. Place 4 muffin cases in each drawer.
5. Select zone 1 and pair it with "BAKE" at 160°C for 15 minutes. Select "MATCH" followed by the "START/STOP" button.
6. Allow your muffins to rest on a cooling rack for about 10 minutes before unmolding and serving.

Sweet Potato Hash

Serves 4

Prep time: 10 minutes / Cook time: 15 minutes

Ingredients

- 600g medium-sized sweet potatoes
- 1/2 medium white onion, diced (or sweet onion)
- 1/2 tsp cayenne pepper
- 1/4 tsp ground cumin
- Sea salt and ground black pepper, to taste
- 50g coconut oil, room temperature

Preparation instructions

1. Remove crisper plates from the drawers. Peel and cut the potatoes into cubes. Now, transfer the potatoes to a bowl and add the onion, spices, and coconut oil.
2. Mix to combine well and divide the mixture between both drawers (without a crisper plate).
3. Select zone 1 and pair it with "AIR FRY" at 200°C for 15 minutes. Select "MATCH" followed by the "START/STOP" button.
4. At the halfway point, turn the hash browns over with silicone-tipped tongs. Reinsert drawers to resume cooking.
5. Serve warm and enjoy!

Traditional English Breakfast

Serves 5

Prep time: 10 minutes / Cook time: 16 minutes

Ingredients

- 250g brown mushrooms, cut into quarters
- 2 small tomatoes, halved
- Sea salt and ground black pepper, to taste
- 1/2 tsp red pepper flakes, crushed
- 5 rashers smoked bacon
- 4 links breakfast sausage
- 100g canned baked beans, drained

Preparation instructions

1. Toss the mushrooms and tomatoes with salt, black pepper, and red pepper. Insert a crisper plate in both drawers. Spray the plates with nonstick cooking oil.
2. Next, add the mushrooms, tomatoes, and bacon to the zone 1 drawer. Add breakfast sausage to the zone 2 drawer.
3. Select zone 1 and pair it with at 180°C for 9 minutes. Select zone 2 and pair it with "AIR FRY" at 200°C for 16 minutes
4. Select "SYNC" followed by the "START/STOP" button. At the halfway point, shake your food or toss it with silicone-tipped tongs to promote even cooking.
5. Place all Ingredients on serving plates and serve with canned beans. You can also add black pudding and fried eggs for a complete English breakfast.
6. Bon appétit!

Herb Garlic Bread

Serves 9

Prep time: 1 hour 30 minutes / Cook time: 30 minutes

Ingredients

- 130ml water warm
- 1 ½ tsp active dry yeast
- 1 ½ tbsp granulated sugar
- 1/2 tsp salt
- 40g butter, melted
- 1 tbsp dried rosemary
- 1 tbsp dried parsley
- 1 tsp dried basil
- 1 garlic clove, minced
- 250g plain flour

Preparation instructions

1. Remove crisper plates from both drawers of your Ninja Foodi.
2. Whisk the water with yeast and sugar in a mixing dish. Allow the mixture to rest for about 10 minutes to activate the yeast.
3. Stir in the salt, 20 grams of butter, herbs, and garlic; beat again to combine well. Add the flour to a large mixing bowl. Now, create a well in the centre, and gradually and slowly stir in the yeast mixture.
4. Mix to combine well. Tip the dough onto a lightly floured work surface and continue kneading your dough until an elastic dough forms.
5. Then, place your dough in a lightly oiled bowl and cover it with a tea towel. Leave to rise for about 1 hour, until doubled in size.
6. Divide your dough in half and place the loaves in two lightly-greased mini loaf tins. Leave to rise for about 20 minutes.
7. Meanwhile, preheat your Ninja Foodi to 165°C for about 5 minutes.
8. Brush the loaves with the remaining 10 grams of melted butter. Add the loaf tins to your Ninja Foodi.
9. Select zone 1 and pair it with "BAKE" at 165°C for 30 minutes. Select "MATCH" followed by the "START/STOP" button.
10. Check the loaves for doneness and let them sit on a cooling rack for about 10 minutes before cutting and serving. Devour!

Italian-Style Frittata

Serves 5

Prep time: 10 minutes / Cook time: 14 minutes

Ingredients

- 8 whole eggs
- 150g double cream
- 1 garlic clove, pressed
- 1 medium scallion stalk, thinly sliced
- 50g bacon bits
- 150g cherry tomatoes, halved
- 1 tbsp Italian herb mix
- 1 tsp red pepper flakes
- Sea salt and ground black pepper, to taste

Preparation instructions

1. Remove a crisper plate from your Ninja Foodi. Line the base of the drawers with baking paper.
2. Preheat the Ninja Foodi to 180°C for 5 minutes.
3. In a bowl, whisk the eggs until frothy; fold in the double cream and mix to combine. Add the other Ingredients and whisk until everything is well incorporated.
4. Spoon the frittata mixture into the prepared drawers.
5. Select zone 1 and pair it with "BAKE" at 180°C for 14 minutes. Select "MATCH" followed by the "START/STOP" button.
6. Cut warm frittata into 5 wedges and serve immediately. Bon appétit!

Easy Breakfast Wraps

Serves 5

Prep time: 10 minutes / Cook time: 21 minutes

Ingredients

- 400g breakfast sausage, sliced
- 500g button mushrooms, cut in quarters
- 1 tsp olive oil
- Sea salt and ground black pepper, to taste
- 1/2 tsp garlic powder
- 5 tortilla wraps
- 1 bell pepper, seeded and sliced
- 100g canned chickpeas, drained

Preparation instructions

1. Insert a crisper plate in both drawers. Spray the plates with nonstick cooking oil.
2. Add breakfast sausage to the zone 1 drawer.
3. Toss the mushrooms with olive oil, salt, black pepper, and garlic powder; now, add the mushrooms to the zone 2 drawer.
4. Select zone 1 and pair it with "AIR FRY" at 200°C for 16 minutes. Select zone 2 and pair it with "AIR FRY" at 200°C for 12 minutes
5. Select "SYNC" followed by the "START/STOP" button. At the halfway point, shake your food or toss it with silicone-tipped tongs to promote even cooking.
6. To assemble your wraps: divide the sausages, mushrooms, pepper, and chickpeas between tortilla wraps; wrap them up.
7. Add wraps to the drawers of your Ninja Foodi. Select "REHEAT" at 170°C for 5 minutes. Devour!

Hot Sandwiches

Serves 5

Prep time: 5 minutes / Cook time: 22 minutes

Ingredients

- 200g Canadian bacon, uncooked
- 500g courgette, cut into 2.5cm slices
- Sea salt and ground black pepper, to taste
- 1/4 tsp cayenne pepper, or more to taste
- 1 tbsp olive oil
- 1 large tomato, sliced
- 1 tbsp English mustard
- 5 medium sandwich buns

Preparation instructions

1. Insert a crisping plate in both drawers. Add bacon to the zone 1 drawer.
2. Toss the courgette with salt, black pepper,

cayenne pepper, and olive oil until the slices are well coated on all sides. Put the courgette slices into the zone 2 drawer.
3. Select zone 1 and pair it with "AIR FRY" at 180°C for 10 minutes. Select zone 2 and pair it with "ROAST" at 200°C for 18 minutes. Select "SYNC" followed by the "START/STOP" button.
4. Divide the bacon, courgette, tomato, and mustard among the sandwich buns.
5. Now, arrange the assembled sandwiches in both drawers in your Ninja Foodi. Select "REHEAT" at 170°C for 4 minutes. Devour!

Yoghurt with Dried Fruit

Serves 9

Prep time: 10 minutes / Cook time: 6 hours

Ingredients

- 2 medium apples, core removed, cut into 3mm slices
- 300g pineapple, peeled, cored, and cut into 3mm slices
- 2 mangoes pit removed, peeled, cut into 3mm slices
- 4 cm ginger root, cut into 3mm slices
- 1L Greek-style yoghurt
- A pinch of ground cinnamon

Preparation instructions

1. Rince the apple slices in lemon water and then, pat them dry with tea towels. Prepare the other fruits.
2. Place a single layer of fruit in the drawer. Then add the crisper plate to the drawer on top of the Ingredients; arrange another layer of fruits on the crisper plate.
3. Select zone 1 and pair it with "DEHYDRATE" at 60°C for 6 hours. Select "MATCH"

followed by the "START/STOP" button.

4. Serve dried fruits with chilled yoghurt. Add a pinch of cinnamon to each serving and enjoy!

Baked Eggs with Vegetables

Serves 6

Prep time: 10 minutes / Cook time: 12 minutes

Ingredients

- 100g double cream
- 2 medium bell peppers, seeded and chopped
- 2 large tomatoes, chopped
- 300ml canned full-fat coconut milk
- 400g spinach
- 1/2 tsp chilli flakes
- 6 whole eggs
- Sea salt and ground black pepper, to taste

Preparation instructions

1. Remove a crisper plate from your Nina Foodi. Preheat the Ninja Foodi to 180°C for 5 minutes.
2. Add the double cream, peppers, tomatoes, milk, spinach, and chilli flakes to a mixing bowl.
3. Divide the mixture between two baking tins; add the tins to the air fryer drawers. Make three holes in each mixture with the back of a tablespoon; now, crack an egg into each hole.
4. Sprinkle the eggs with salt and black pepper.
5. Select zone 1 and pair it with "BAKE" at 180°C for 12 minutes. Select "MATCH" followed by the "START/STOP" button.
6. Bon appétit!

Breakfast Brownies

Serves 8

Prep time: 10 minutes / Cook time: 40 minutes

Ingredients

- 200g cups quick oats
- 50g brown sugar
- 1 tbsp cocoa powder
- 1 tbsp flaxseed meal
- 1/4 tsp cinnamon powder
- 120ml unsweetened applesauce
- 1 egg, beaten
- 350ml coconut milk
- 40g dark chocolate chunks

Preparation instructions

1. Remove a crisper plate from your Nina Foodi. Line the zone 1 and 2 drawers with a piece of baking paper.
2. In a mixing bowl, thoroughly combine the oats, sugar, cocoa powder, flaxseed meal, and cinnamon powder.
3. Then, gradually and slowly, stir in the applesauce, egg, and coconut milk; mix until creamy and uniform. Fold in the chocolate chunks and whisk to combine well.
4. Spoon the batter into the prepared drawers.
5. Select zone 1 and pair it with "BAKE" at 160°C for 40 minutes. Select "MATCH" followed by the "START/STOP" button.
6. Check your brownies with a toothpick; allow your brownies to rest on a cooling rack for about 10 minutes before cutting and serving.
7. Bon appétit!

Breakfast Crunchy Cereals

Serves 7

Prep time: 5 minutes / Cook time: 15 minutes

Ingredients

- 200g rolled oats
- 100g pumpkin seeds
- 100g peanut butter

- 30g hemp seeds
- 60g almonds, slivered
- 100g agave syrup
- 1/2 tsp ground cloves
- 1/2 tsp ground cinnamon
- 30g sesame seeds

Preparation instructions

1. Begin by preheating your Ninja Foodi to 170°C.
2. In a mixing bowl, thoroughly combine rolled oats, pumpkin seeds, peanut butter, hemp seeds, almonds, agave syrup, ground cloves, and cinnamon.
3. Spoon the mixture into two parchment-lined roasting tins; press down slightly using a silicone spatula. Place the baking tins in both drawers.
4. Select zone 1 and pair it with "BAKE" at 170°C for 15 minutes. Select "MATCH" followed by the "START/STOP" button.
5. When zone 1 time reaches 8 minutes, add sesame seeds, and reinsert the drawer to continue cooking.
6. Let your cereals cool before serving and storing. Enjoy!

Baked Burrata Bruschetta

Serves 6

Prep time: 5 minutes / Cook time: 4 minutes

Ingredients

- 1 loaf of crusty bread, sliced
- 500g cherry tomatoes, halved
- 1 large garlic clove, peeled
- 30ml extra-virgin olive oil
- 1 tbsp chardonnay vinegar
- Sea salt and ground black pepper, to taste
- 100g broad beans, double podded, blanched

- 1 large burrata, at room temperature and sliced
- 1 small pack fresh mint, chopped
- 1 small pack fresh parsley, chopped

Preparation instructions

1. Place bread slices in zone 1 and zone 2 drawers. Select zone 1 and pair it with "BAKE" at 180°C for 2 minutes. Select "MATCH" to duplicate settings across both zones. Press the "START/STOP" button.
2. Meanwhile, toss cherry tomatoes with garlic, olive oil, vinegar, salt, black pepper, and beans.
3. Top the bread slices with tomato mixture and arrange them in both drawers.
4. Select zone 1 and pair it with "BAKE" at 180°C for 2 minutes. Select "MATCH" to duplicate settings across both zones. Press the "START/STOP" button.
5. Garnish your bruschetta with fresh burrata, mint, and basil leaves.
6. Bon appétit!

Breakfast Bars

Serves 12

Prep time: 5 minutes / Cook time: 15 minutes

Ingredients

- 60g raisins
- 20g sunflower seed
- 20g pumpkin seeds
- 150g oats
- 30g multi-grain hoop cereal
- 100g coconut oil, softened
- 100g brown sugar
- 100g honey

Preparation instructions

1. Begin by preheating your Ninja Foodi to 180°C.

2. In a mixing bowl, thoroughly combine all Ingredients until everything is well combined.
3. Spoon the mixture into two parchment-lined roasting tins; press down the mixture with a wide spatula. Place the baking tins in both drawers.
4. Select zone 1 and pair it with "BAKE" at 180°C for 15 minutes. Select "MATCH" followed by the "START/STOP" button.
5. Let it cool before slicing it into bars.
6. Bon appétit!

Full English Breakfast

Serves 2

Prep time: 5 minutes / Cook time: 20-25 minutes

Ingredients

- 4 sausages
- 2 slices of bread
- 4 slices of bacon
- 2 eggs
- 2 slices of black pudding
- 1 tomato, halved
- 4 mushrooms
- Salt and pepper, to taste

Preparation instructions

1. Preheat the Ninja Foodi air fryer to 200°C.
2. Place the sausages, bacon, black pudding, mushrooms, and tomato in the air fryer basket.
3. Cook for 15-20 minutes, flipping the items halfway through.
4. While the breakfast items are cooking, toast the bread and fry the eggs on a skillet.
5. Serve the cooked items with the toast and eggs. Season with salt and pepper to taste.

Mini Blueberry Scones

Serves 8

Prep time: 15 minutes / Cook time: 15 minutes

Ingredients

- 250 ml all-purpose flour
- 4 tablespoons white sugar, divided
- 1 ½ teaspoons baking powder
- ⅛ teaspoon baking soda
- ⅛ teaspoon salt
- 2 tablespoons butter
- 1 egg
- 60 ml buttermilk
- ½ teaspoon vanilla extract
- 60 ml fresh blueberries
- 2 teaspoons orange zest

Preparation instructions

1. Preheat the Ninja Foodi air fryer to 180 °C.
2. Stir together flour, 2 tablespoons sugar, baking powder, baking soda, and salt in a medium bowl. Cut in butter with two knives or pastry blender until mixture resembles coarse crumbs.
3. Beat egg with a fork in a small bowl. Remove 2 tablespoons egg to another small bowl; set aside. Add buttermilk and vanilla extract to remaining egg; whisk with the fork until combined. Stir into flour mixture until just moistened. Gently stir in blueberries.
4. Transfer dough to a lightly floured surface. Gently knead until dough is no longer sticky, about 8 to 10 strokes. Pat dough into a 6-inch circle. Cut into 8 wedges, without separating, dipping the knife in flour between cuts.
5. Combine remaining 2 tablespoons sugar and orange zest in a small bowl. Brush top of dough with reserved egg and sprinkle with

sugar mixture. Separate dough wedges and carefully arrange them, using a small wide spatula, in a single layer in the fryer basket, in batches if necessary.

6. Cook scones until golden brown, about 6 minutes. Serve warm.

Air Fryer Cheese Swirls

Serves 6

Prep time: 12 minutes / Cook time: 12 minutes

Ingredients
- 2 Tbsp Mustard
- ½ Small Onion diced
- 150 g Grated Cheese
- Egg Wash
- Scone Dough
- 225 g Self Raising Flour
- 50 g Butter
- 120 ml Semi Skimmed Milk
- 28 g Grated Cheese
- 1 Tbsp Parsley
- Salt & Pepper

Preparation instructions
1. Rub the fat into the flour until it resembles breadcrumbs. Add your seasoning and 28g of grated cheese. Then use enough milk to make a scone dough.
2. Add flour to a clean worktop and to your rolling pin. Roll out your dough into big rectangle shape. Brush the edges with mustard.
3. Then add diced onion and grated cheese.
4. Gradually roll it from the top, adding some egg wash as you go so that it will stick together as it rolls.
5. Once it is fully rolled add to a chopping board and slice into medium slices.

6. Place a layer of foil in the Ninja Foodi air fryer, then add the sliced cheese whirls and then air fry for 6 minutes at 160°C followed by 6 more minutes at 140°C.

Potato Pancakes

Serves 4-6

Prep time: 10 minutes / Cook time: 9 minutes

Ingredients
- 750 g of shredded hash browns
- 1 teaspoon of paprika
- Salt and pepper to taste
- 32 ml of all purpose flour
- 1 egg
- 2-3 green onions
- 1 teaspoon of garlic

Preparation instructions
1. In a large bowl, combine the hash browns that have been shredded, the garlic, paprika, salt, pepper, flour, and egg.
2. Only the green portion of your green onions should be chopped, and then mix them in with the other Ingredients.
3. Turn on the Ninja foodi air fryer and heat it to 370 degrees.
4. Make your pancakes while it's cooking up. Spooned the mixture into a measuring cup with a 32 ml capacity. Shook it out after that, and it took the shape of a measuring cup. To shape the mixture into a pancake, merely applied pressure. Spray your basket's bottom liberally once your air fryer is ready. The basket should include your potato cakes. Avoid packing it too tightly because you'll need space to rotate them halfway through the cooking process.
5. After 4 minutes, turn the food. Your potato

pancakes should cook for a further 4-5 minutes after being sprayed on top.

6. If preferred, top with more green onions and sour cream before serving.

Air fryer cheese bread puffs

Makes 32

Prep time: 20 minutes / Cook time: 1h 15 minutes

Ingredients

- 250ml milk
- 125ml vegetable oil
- 300g tapioca flour
- 2 eggs
- 70g finely grated parmesan cheese

Preparation instructions

1. In a saucepan, boil the milk and oil over medium heat for 2 minutes, or until the milk simmers. Add the flour and blend by stirring. Mixture should be transferred to a stand mixer's bowl. Beat for two minutes, or until smooth and slightly chilled.

2. One at a time, beat thoroughly after each addition before adding the eggs. Just mix the cheese after adding it. Make balls out of tablespoons of batter using wet hands.

3. Baking paper should be trimmed to suit the base of Ninja foodi air fryer basket. Place the balls on the baking paper 5 cm apart. 15 minutes of cooking at 180°C or until golden and puffy. the remaining balls, then repeat. Serve.

Omelette with Spinach and Peppers

Serves 4

Prep time: 10 minutes / Cook time: 13 minutes

Ingredients

- 7 whole eggs
- 100g double cream
- 1 medium onion, peeled and chopped
- 1 medium bell pepper, deseeded and chopped
- 2 cups baby spinach
- Sea salt and ground black pepper, to taste

Preparation instructions

1. Remove a crisper plate from your Nina Foodi. Very lightly butter two baking tins.

2. In a mixing bowl, thoroughly combine all the Ingredients.

3. Spoon the mixture into the prepared baking tins. Place the tins in the prepared drawers.

4. Select zone 1 and pair it with "BAKE" at 180°C for 13 minutes. Select "MATCH" followed by the "START/STOP" button. Bon appétit!

CHAPTER 2 BEANS & GRAINS

BBQ Millet Patties

Serves 4

Prep time: 10 minutes / Cook time: 20 minutes

Ingredients

- 300g millet, soaked overnight and rinsed
- 1 (400g) can red kidney beans, rinsed and drained
- 1 tbsp fresh mint
- 1 tbsp fresh parsley
- 2 garlic cloves
- 1 large onion, chopped
- 100g breadcrumbs
- Sea salt and ground black pepper, to taste
- 100g BBQ sauce

Preparation instructions

1. Insert the crisper plates in both drawers and spray them with cooking oil.
2. In your blender or food processor, mix all the Ingredients until a thick and uniform batter is formed. Shape the mixture into 8 equal patties.
3. Now, spray the patties with nonstick cooking oil and then, place them in the prepared drawers.
4. Select zone 1 and pair it with "AIR FRY" at 190°C for 20 minutes. Select "MATCH" to duplicate settings across both zones. Press the "START/STOP" button.
5. When zone 1 time reaches 10 minutes, turn the patties over and spray them with cooking oil on the other side; then, reinsert the drawers to continue cooking.
6. Bon appétit!

Crunchy Granola

Serves 8

Prep time: 5 minutes / Cook time: 15 minutes

Ingredients

- 200g rolled oats
- 100g walnuts, roughly chopped
- 50g coconut oil
- 100g honey
- 80g pumpkin seeds
- 30g hemp seeds
- 50g walnuts, roughly chopped
- 1/2 tsp ground cloves
- 1 tsp ground cinnamon

Preparation instructions

1. Begin by preheating your Ninja Foodi to 180°C. Line two roasting tins that fit in your Ninja Foodi with baking paper.
2. Mix the oats, walnuts, coconut oil, and 50g of honey. Spread the mixture onto a roasting tin and add the roasting tin to the zone 1 drawer.
3. Mix the remaining Ingredients, spread the mixture onto a roasting tin and add it to the zone 2 drawer.
4. Select zone 1 and pair it with "ROAST" at 170°C for 15 minutes. Select zone 2 and pair it with "ROAST
5. When zone 1 time reaches 8 minutes, stir the Ingredients, and reinsert the drawer to continue cooking.
6. When zone 2 time reaches 5 minutes, stir the Ingredients, and reinsert the drawer to continue cooking.
7. Add the oat/nut mixture to the seed mixture and stir to combine well; let your granola cool before serving and storing. Enjoy!

Polenta Fries with Green Beans

Serves 4

Prep time: 5 minutes / Cook time: 18 minutes

Ingredients

- 500g polenta log
- 2 tsp olive oil
- Sea salt and ground black pepper, to taste
- 1 tsp cayenne pepper
- 1 tsp dried oregano
- 500g green beans, trimmed

Preparation instructions

1. Cut the polenta log into fries and drizzle them with 1 teaspoon of olive oil. Sprinkle polenta fries with salt, black pepper, cayenne pepper, and oregano.
2. Insert a crisper plate into the zone 1 drawer. Spray the crisper plate with nonstick cooking oil.
3. Toss green beans with the remaining 1 teaspoon of olive oil, salt, and black pepper to your liking.
4. Place the polenta fries in the zone 1 drawer. Place the green beans in the zone 2 drawer (with no crisper plate inserted).
5. Select zone 1 and pair it with "AIR FRY" at 185°C for 18 minutes. Select zone 2 and pair it with "ROAST" at 200°C for 8 minutes. Select "SYNC" followed by the "START/STOP" button.
6. When zone 1 time reaches 9 minutes, turn the polenta fries over and reinsert the drawer to continue cooking.
7. When zone 2 time reaches 4 minutes, toss the drawer to ensure even cooking; reinsert the drawer to continue cooking.
8. Serve polenta fries with fried green beans on the side and enjoy!

Autumn Oat Bake

Serves 7

Prep time: 10 minutes / Cook time: 20 minutes

Ingredients

- 400g old-fashioned oats
- 2 tsp coconut oil, melted
- 2 small eggs, beaten
- 1 ½ cups full-fat coconut milk
- 2 small apples, cored, peeled, and sliced
- 1 tsp baking powder
- 1/2 cup honey
- A pinch of ground cinnamon
- 1 tsp vanilla bean paste
- A pinch of grated nutmeg

Preparation instructions

1. Brush the inside of two oven-safe baking tins with coconut oil. Thoroughly combine all the Ingredients and spoon the mixture into the baking tins.
2. Select zone 1 and pair it with "BAKE" at 190°C for 20 minutes. Select "MATCH" to duplicate settings across both zones. Press the "START/STOP" button.
3. When zone 1 time reaches 10 minutes, turn the baking tins and reinsert the drawers to continue cooking.
4. Bon appétit!

Jacket Potato with Baked Beans

Serves 4

Prep time: 5 minutes / Cook time: 35-45 minutes

Ingredients

- 1 large potato
- 1/2 can of baked beans

- 1/4 cup grated cheese
- Salt and pepper, to taste

Preparation instructions

1. Preheat the air fryer to 400°F.
2. Pierce the potato with a fork all over.
3. Place the potato in the air fryer basket.
4. Cook for 35-45 minutes, until crispy on the outside and soft on the inside.
5. Heat up the baked beans in a microwave-safe dish for 1-2 minutes.
6. Cut open the potato and fluff the insides with a fork.
7. Pour the heated baked beans over the potato and sprinkle with grated cheese, salt, and pepper.
8. Cook in the air fryer for 2-3 minutes, until the cheese is melted. Serve hot.

Rustic Qinoa Porridge

Serves 4

Prep time: 10 minutes / Cook time: 15 minutes

Ingredients

- 2 tsp coconut oil, melted
- 350g quinoa, soaked overnight and rinsed
- 1 tbsp cocoa powder
- 100g dried apricots, pitted and chopped
- 2 large bananas, peeled and mashed
- 1 litre milk
- 1 vanilla bean, split
- 1 cinnamon stick

Preparation instructions

1. Brush the inside of two oven-safe baking tins with coconut oil.
2. Mix the quinoa with the other Ingredients and spoon the mixture into the baking tins. Add the baking tins to the drawers.

3. Select zone 1 and pair it with "BAKE" at 180°C for 15 minutes. Select "MATCH" to duplicate settings across both zones. Press the "START/STOP" button.
4. When zone 1 time reaches 7 minutes, rotate both baking tins and reinsert the drawers to continue cooking.
5. Bon appétit!

Buckwheat & Garbanzo Bean Burgers

Serves 6

Prep time: 10 minutes / Cook time: 20 minutes

Ingredients

- 1 (400g) can garbanzo beans, rinsed and drained
- 200g buckwheat, soaked overnight, drained and rinsed
- 1 large onion, chopped
- 2 medium garlic cloves, minced
- 100g breadcrumbs
- Sea salt and ground black pepper, to taste
- 1 tsp smoked paprika
- 1/2 tsp cumin seeds
- 150ml BBQ sauce

Preparation instructions

1. Insert the crisper plates in both drawers and spray them with cooking oil.
2. In your blender or a food processor, thoroughly combine all the Ingredients. Shape the mixture into 6 patties and spray them with nonstick cooking oil. Now, arrange them in the lightly-greased drawers.
3. Select zone 1 and pair it with "AIR FRY" at 190°C for 20 minutes. Select "MATCH" to duplicate settings across both zones. Press the "START/STOP" button.

4. When zone 1 time reaches 10 minutes, turn the burgers over, spray them with cooking oil on the other side, and reinsert the drawers to continue cooking.

5. Serve burger patties in hamburger buns with toppings of choice.

6. Bon appétit!

Bolognese Pasta Bake

Serves 6

Prep time: 10 minutes / Cook time: 21 minutes

Ingredients

- 400g pasta of choice
- 1 tbsp olive oil
- 600g turkey mince
- 1 medium leek, chopped
- 2 small garlic cloves, crushed
- 2 (400g) cans tomatoes, chopped
- 1 large bell pepper, seeded and chopped
- 300ml chicken stock
- 100g canned white beans, drained and rinsed
- 1 tbsp Italian herb mix
- 400g cheddar cheese, shredded

Preparation instructions

1. Remove a crisper plate from your Ninja Foodi. Brush two baking tins with nonstick oil.

2. Cook pasta according to the manufacturer's instructions.

3. Meanwhile, heat olive oil in a nonstick frying pan over medium-high heat. Cook turkey mince for about 3 minutes, until no longer pink.

4. In the same pan, sauté the leek for about 3 minutes, until tender and translucent; add garlic and continue sauteing for 30 seconds more, until aromatic.

5. Add the turkey mixture to the pasta; stir

in the chopped tomatoes, pepper, chicken stock, beans, and Italian herbs. Spoon the mixture into prepared baking tins and add the tins to your Ninja Foodi.

6. Select zone 1 and pair it with "BAKE" at 180°C for 15 minutes. Select "MATCH" followed by the "START/STOP" button.

7. When zone 1 time reaches 10 minutes, top each casserole with cheese; reinsert the drawers to continue cooking.

8. Bon appétit!

Classic Baked Risotto

Serves 6

Prep time: 10 minutes / Cook time: 21 minutes

Ingredients

- 1 tbsp butter, room temperature
- 250g bacon rashers, chopped into small pieces
- 1 onion, chopped
- 350g risotto rice
- 1 medium tomato puree
- 700ml beef bone stock
- 60g parmesan, grated

Preparation instructions

1. Remove a crisper plate from your Ninja Foodi. Lightly butter two baking tins and set them aside.

2. Preheat a frying pan over medium-high heat; then, cook the bacon until crisp, stirring continuously.

3. Then, saute the onion for about 3 minutes, until translucent. Divide the sauteed mixture between two baking tins.

4. Tip in the rice; pour over the tomato puree and stock. Add baking tins to the drawers.

5. Select zone 1 and pair it with "BAKE" at 180°C for 18 minutes. Select "MATCH" to

duplicate settings across both zones. Press the "START/STOP" button.

6. At the halfway point, stir your risotto with a wooden spoon and reinsert the drawers to resume cooking.

7. Top hot risotto with parmesan cheese and serve immediately. Bon appétit!

Cornbread Muffins

Serves 6

Prep time: 10 minutes / Cook time: 25 minutes

Ingredients

- 50g butter, melted
- 2 scallion stalks, chopped
- 100g sweetcorn kernels
- 2 small eggs
- 50ml milk
- 140ml pot buttermilk
- 80g plain flour
- 80g polenta or cornmeal
- 1 tsp baking powder
- 30g Swiss cheese, grated

Preparation instructions

1. Remove a crisper plate from your Ninja Foodi. Lightly spray muffin cases with cooking oil.

2. Melt the butter in a frying pan over medium-low heat; cook scallion and corn kernels for approximately 5 minutes, until soft.

3. Add the other Ingredients and gently stir to combine. Spoon the mixture into the prepared muffin cases.

4. Add muffin cases to both drawers.

5. Select zone 1 and pair it with "BAKE" at 180°C for 25 minutes, until golden brown. Select "MATCH" to duplicate settings across both zones. Press the "START/STOP"

button.

Nutty Millet Bake

Serves 5

Prep time: 10 minutes / Cook time: 28 minutes

Ingredients

- 2 tsp butter, melted
- 350g millet, rinsed
- 1 litre milk
- 100g prunes, pitted and chopped
- 2 eggs, beaten
- 120g almonds, chopped
- 1/2 tsp vanilla bean paste
- 1/2 tsp ground cinnamon
- 1/2 tsp grated nutmeg (optional)

Preparation instructions

1. Remove a crisper plate from your Ninja Foodi. Brush two oven-safe baking tins with the melted butter.

2. Tip the millet into a deep saucepan and pour in the milk; add 350ml of water and bring it to a boil. Reduce the heat to medium-low; leave to simmer for 13 to 15 minutes, stirring continuously, until the millet is tender.

3. Mix the millet with the other Ingredients and spoon the mixture into the prepared baking tins. Add the baking tins to the drawers.

4. Select zone 1 and pair it with "BAKE" at 180°C for 13 minutes. Select "MATCH" to duplicate settings across both zones. Press the "START/STOP" button.

5. When zone 1 time reaches 6 minutes, rotate both baking tins and reinsert the drawers to continue cooking.

6. Bon appétit!

French Toast with Roasted Beans

Serves 4

Prep time: 10 minutes / Cook time: 15 minutes

Ingredients
- 2 medium eggs
- 4 tbsp double cream
- 1 tbsp golden syrup
- 2 tbsp butter, room temperature
- 4 thick whole-grain bread slices
- 120g canned kidney beans, drained and rinsed

Preparation instructions
1. Spray crisper plates with cooking oil. Preheat the Ninja Foodi to 180°C for 5 minutes.
2. In a mixing bowl, whisk the eggs, cream, syrup, and butter. Dip bread slices in the custard mixture until they are well coated on all sides. Place French toast in the zone 1 drawer. Add kidney beans to the zone 2 drawer.
3. Select zone 1 and pair it with "AIR FRYER" at 180°C for 13 to 15 minutes. Select zone 2 and pair it with "ROAST" at 180°C for 10 minutes. Select "SYNC" followed by the "START/STOP" button.
4. When zone 1 time reaches 7 minutes, turn the French toast over and reinsert the drawer to continue cooking.
5. When zone 2 time reaches 5 minutes, toss the drawer and reinsert the drawer to continue cooking.
6. Serve French toast with roasted beans. Bon appétit!

Naan with Refried Beans

Serves 4

Prep time: 1 hour 15 minutes / Cook time: 10 minutes

Ingredients
- Naan:
- 60ml warm water
- 1/2 tsp dried yeast
- 1 tsp golden caster sugar
- 150g strong white bread flour
- 15g butter
- 75ml yoghurt
- Refried Beans:
- 1 tbsp olive oil
- 1/2 tsp cayenne pepper
- Sea salt and ground black pepper, to taste
- 4 clove garlic, pressed
- 1/2 tsp chilli powder
- 1/2 can (425g) pinto beans with onion, rinsed and drained
- 1 tbsp fresh coriander, chopped

Preparation instructions
1. Remove crisper plates from your Ninja Foodi. Line the zone 1 drawer with baking paper.
2. Whisk the water with yeast and sugar in a mixing dish; let the mixture sit for about 10 minutes to activate the yeast.
3. Add the prepared yeast to the flour; add the butter and yoghurt and mix to combine well. Knead the dough until smooth and satin-like dough forms.
4. After that, shape the dough into a ball and place it in the bowl. Cover and leave the dough in a warm place for about 1 hour, until doubled in size.
5. Divide the dough into 4 balls and flatten them using your hands. Add naan to the zone 1 drawer and brush with olive oil.

6. In a baking tin, thoroughly combine all Ingredients for the refried beans. Add the baking tin to the zone 2 drawer.

7. Select zone 1 and pair it with "BAKE" at 180°C for 10 minutes. Select zone 2 and pair it with "BAKE" at 180°C for 10 minutes. Select "SYNC" followed by the "START/STOP" button. Work in batches, if needed.

8. When zone 1 time reaches 5 minutes, turn the naan bread over, spray with olive oil on the other side, and reinsert the drawer to continue cooking.

9. Serve warm naan bread with refried beans and enjoy!

Chinese Fried Rice

Serves 5

Prep time: 10 minutes / Cook time: 19 minutes

Ingredients

- 2 tsp toasted sesame oil
- 1 onion, chopped
- 300g rice, cooked and chilled
- 2 large eggs, whisked
- 2 tbsp soy sauce
- 200g broccoli, broken into small florets
- 1 medium carrot, trimmed and chopped
- 200g tofu, pressed and cubed

Preparation instructions

1. Remove a crisper plate from the zone 1 drawer. Lightly spray a baking tin with nonstick cooking oil.

2. Heat 1 teaspoon of sesame oil in a frying pan over medium-high heat. Saute the onion for about 3 minutes, until just tender.

3. Tip in the rice; add the eggs, 1 tbsp of soy sauce, broccoli, and carrot, and stir to combine. Spoon the mixture into the baking

tin and add it to the zone 1 drawer.

4. Brush tofu cubes with the remaining 1 teaspoon of sesame oil and 1 tablespoon of soy sauce; place them in the zone 2 drawer (with a crisper plate).

5. Select zone 1 and pair it with "BAKE" at 180°C for 16 minutes. Select zone 2 and pair it with "ROAST" at 190°C for 15 minutes. Select "SYNC" followed by the "START/STOP" button.

6. When zone 1 time reaches 8 minutes, stir your rice to ensure even cooking; reinsert the drawer to continue cooking.

7. When zone 2 time reaches 8 minutes, shake the drawer to ensure even cooking; reinsert the drawer to continue cooking.

8. Devour!

Green Beans with Almonds

Serves 4

Prep time: 5 minutes / Cook time: 10 minutes

Ingredients

- 800g green beans, ends trimmed
- 2 tsp olive oil
- 1 tsp cayenne pepper
- 1 tsp dried dill weed (optional)
- Sea salt and ground black pepper, to taste
- 80g almonds, whole

Preparation instructions

1. Insert a crisper plate into the zone 1 and zone 2 drawers. Spray the crisper plate with nonstick cooking oil.

2. Toss green beans and almonds with the other Ingredients.

3. Select zone 1 and pair it with "AIR FRY" at 200°C for 10 minutes. Select "MATCH" to duplicate settings across both zones. Press

the "START/STOP" button.

4. When zone 1 time reaches 10 minutes, toss the drawers and reinsert them to continue cooking.

5. Bon appétit!

Quinoa & Bean Patties in Tortilla

Serves 4

Prep time: 10 minutes / Cook time: 24 minutes

Ingredients

- Patties:
- 150g quinoa, soaked overnight and rinsed
- 1/2 (200) can red kidney beans, rinsed and drained
- 1 tbsp fresh parsley
- 2 garlic cloves
- 1 medium onion, chopped
- 60g rolled oats
- Sea salt and ground black pepper, to taste
- 2 tbsp hot ketchup
- 1 tsp smoked paprika
- Tortilla:
- 500g courgette, cut into 2.5cm slices
- 1 tsp olive oil
- 4 whole-wheat tortillas

Preparation instructions

1. Insert a crisper plate in the zone 1 drawer and spray it with cooking oil.

2. In your blender or food processor, mix all the Ingredients for the patties until a thick and uniform batter is formed.

3. Shape the mixture into 4 equal patties. Now, spray the patties with nonstick cooking oil and then, place them in the zone 1 drawer.

4. Toss courgette slices with 1 teaspoon of olive oil. Add courgette slices to the zone 2 drawer.

5. Select zone 1 and pair it with "AIR FRY" at 180°C for 20 minutes. Select zone 2 and pair it with "ROAST" at 200°C for 16 minutes. Select "SYNC" followed by the "START/ STOP" button.

6. When zone 1 time reaches 10 minutes, turn the patties over and spray them with cooking oil on the other side; then, reinsert the drawer to continue cooking.

7. When zone 2 time reaches 8 minutes, toss the drawer, and reinsert it to continue cooking.

8. Place tortillas in both drawers in your Ninja Foodi. Select "REHEAT" at 170°C for 4 minutes.

9. Add patties and courgette slices to warmed tortillas and roll them up. Bon appétit!

Chunky Oven Chips with Breaded Mushrooms

Serves 4

Prep time: 10 minutes / Cook time: 15 minutes

Ingredients

- 500g potatoes, peeled and cut into thick slices
- 1/2 tsp garlic granules
- 1 tsp olive oil
- Sea salt and ground black pepper, to your liking
- 400g button mushrooms
- 60g breadcrumbs

Preparation instructions

1. Insert a crisper plate into the zone 1 and zone 2 drawers. Spray the crisper plate with nonstick cooking oil.
2. Toss potato slices with garlic granules, olive oil, and salt. Place the potatoes in the zone 1 drawer.
3. Toss button mushrooms with breadcrumbs, salt, and black pepper. Place the mushrooms in the zone 2 drawer.
4. Select zone 1 and pair it with "AIR FRY" at 180°C for 15 minutes. Select "MATCH" to duplicate settings across both zones. Press the "START/STOP" button.
5. When zone 1 time reaches 8 minutes, shake both drawers; then, reinsert the drawers to continue cooking.
6. Enjoy!

Chicken Breasts with Cheesy Cauliflower

Serves 3

Prep time: 10 minutes / Cook time: 33 minutes

Ingredients

- 500g chicken breasts, boneless, skinless, cut into 3 pieces
- 600g cauliflower, cut into 2.5cm florets
- 2 tsp olive oil
- 1/2 tsp garlic granules
- Sea salt and ground black pepper, to taste
- 100g parmesan cheese, grated

Preparation instructions

1. Insert crisper plate in both drawers. Toss chicken breasts and cauliflower florets with olive oil, garlic granules, salt, and black pepper.
2. Spray the crisper plates with nonstick cooking oil. Place the chicken breasts in the zone 1 drawer and the cauliflower florets in the zone 2 drawer.
3. Select zone 1 and pair it with "AIR FRY" at 190°C for 33 minutes. Select zone 2 and pair it with "AIR FRY" at 200°C for 20 minutes. Select "SYNC" followed by the "START/STOP" button.
4. At the halfway point, flip the Ingredients with silicone-tipped tongs to promote even cooking. Add cheese and reinsert drawers to resume cooking.
5. Bon appétit!

Holiday Roast

Serves 4

Prep time: 10 minutes + marinating time / Cook time: 1 hour

Ingredients

- 800g Boston butt, cut into 4 pieces

Marinade:

- 100ml dry red wine
- 1 tbsp Dijon mustard

- 1 tbsp hot paprika
- 50ml tomato sauce
- Sea salt and ground black pepper
- 2 tbsp olive oil

Preparation instructions

1. Mix all the marinade Ingredients. Add Boston butt to the marinade and let it sit for about 1 hour in your fridge.
2. Insert crisper plates in both drawers. Spray the crisper plates with nonstick cooking oil.
3. Remove the Boston butt from the marinade. Place the Boston butt in both drawers. Select zone 1 and pair it with "AIR FRY" at 175°C for 55 minutes to 1 hour. Select "MATCH" to duplicate settings across both zones. Press the "START/STOP" button.
4. At the halfway point, turn the Boston butt over, brush them with the reserved marinade and reinsert the drawers to resume cooking.
5. Enjoy!

Traditional Fajitas

Serves 4

Prep time: 10 minutes / Cook time: 45 minutes

Ingredients

- 2 (200g each) turkey fillets, skinless, boneless, cut into strips
- 2 large bell pepper, deseeded and sliced
- 1 small chilli pepper, sliced
- 1 medium onion, peeled and sliced
- 2 tbsp olive oil
- 1 tsp dried Mexican oregano
- Sea salt and freshly ground black pepper, to taste
- 4 medium tortillas

Preparation instructions

1. Insert crisper plates in both drawers. Spray

the crisper plates with nonstick cooking oil.
2. Toss turkey breasts, both peppers, and onion with olive oil and spices.
3. Place the turkey breasts in the zone 1 drawer and the vegetables in the zone 2 drawer.
4. Select zone 1 and pair it with "AIR FRY" at 175°C for 40 minutes. Select zone 2 and pair it with "AIR FRY" at 200°C for 16 minutes. Select "SYNC" followed by the "START/STOP" button.
5. Flip the Ingredients once or twice to promote even cooking. Reinsert drawers to resume cooking. (If the turkey has not reached an internal temperature of 73°c, set it for another 5 or 10 minutes).
6. Add tortillas to both drawers. Select "REHEAT" at 170°C for 5 minutes.
7. Add the turkey to the warmed tortillas; top them with onions and bell peppers. Enjoy!

Sunday Roast with Classic Roast Potatoes

Serves 6

Prep time: 10 minutes / Cook time: 16-18 minutes

Ingredients

- 1 tbsp loosely packed fresh rosemary leaves
- 1/2 – 1 tbsp olive oil
- 1–2 tbsp unsalted butter
- kosher salt
- 1 tsp black or pink peppercorns
- 1–1.4 kg eye of round roast
- classic roast potatoes
- Horseradish Cream Ingredients
- 70 g sour cream
- 1 1/2 tbsp prepared horseradish
- kosher salt
- 1 tbsp honey

Preparation instructions

1. Grind the rosemary, 1 1/2 teaspoons salt, and the peppercorns in a mortar and pestle or in a small bowl using the handle of a wooden spoon. It should be a thick mixture. With paper towels, pat the roast to dry. Depending on the size of the roast, rub 1/2 to 1 tablespoon of oil all over the meat before seasoning it on all sides.

2. Spray canola oil on the Ninja foodi air fryer basket. Put the roast in the basket's middle. Attach the air fryer cover after placing the basket within the pot. Press the Air Fry button and adjust the cooking temperature to 325°F (165°C) for 16 to 18 minutes per kilogram of beef (start with the lower amount of time and add more time if needed).

3. Make the horseradish cream in the meantime by combining the sour cream, horseradish, and 1/4 teaspoon salt in a small bowl. Salt the dish to taste and correct the seasoning. When not in use, cover and place in the fridge.

4. When the specified cooking time has passed, place an instant-read thermometer into the center of the meat; for medium, the reading should be between 135 and 145 degrees Fahrenheit (57 and 63 degrees Celsius). If the roast is not done to your liking, continue cooking it for an additional 2 minutes at a time. The roast should be moved to a chopping board using tongs. Depending on the size of the roast, place 1-2 teaspoons of butter on top and let it to melt. Drizzle with the honey, loosely cover with foil, and allow to rest for 15 to 20 minutes.

Fish with Roasted Sweet Potatoes

Serves 4

Prep time: 10 minutes / Cook time: 20 minutes

Ingredients

- 4 (170g each) cod fillets, skinless
- 650g potatoes, peeled and cut into 2.5cm chunks
- 1 tbsp paprika
- 1 tsp dried basil
- Sea salt and ground black pepper, to taste
- 1 medium lemon, freshly squeezed
- 1 tsp olive oil

Preparation instructions

1. Pat cod fillets dry using tea towels. Toss cod fillets with paprika, basil, salt and pepper. Drizzle the fish and potatoes with lemon juice and olive oil.

2. Add cod fillets to the zone 1 drawer and potatoes to the zone 2 drawer.

3. Select zone 1 and pair it with "ROAST" at 200°C for 13 minutes. Select zone 2 and pair it with "AIR FRY" at 200°C for 20 minutes. Select "SYNC" followed by the "START/ STOP" button.

4. When zone 1 time reaches 7 minutes, turn the fish fillets over using silicone-tipped tongs. Reinsert the drawer to continue cooking.

5. When zone 2 time reaches 10 minutes, shake the drawer for a few seconds to promote even cooking. Reinsert the drawer to continue cooking.

6. Taste and adjust the seasonings. Garnish warm fish with potatoes and serve immediately!

Chicken Tenders with Carrots

Serves 4

Prep time: 5 minutes / Cook time: 22 minutes

Ingredients

- 1 bay leaf
- 1 thyme sprig, leaves picked

- 1 rosemary sprig, leaves picked
- 1 garlic clove, minced
- 500g frozen chicken tenders
- 1 tsp butter, melted
- Sea salt and ground black pepper, to taste
- 500g carrots, cut into 1.5 slices
- 1 tsp olive oil

Preparation instructions

1. Insert crisper plates in both drawers. Spray the crisper plates with nonstick cooking oil.
2. Crush the bay leaf, thyme, rosemary leaves, and garlic in a pestle and mortar; reserve.
3. Toss chicken tenders with 1 teaspoon of melted butter, crushed spice, salt, and black pepper. Now, toss carrots with olive oil, salt, and pepper.
4. Place the chicken tenders in the zone 1 drawer and the carrots in the zone 2 drawer.
5. Select zone 1 and pair it with "AIR FRY" at 200°C for 22 minutes. Select zone 2 and pair it with "ROAST" at 200°C for 16 minutes. Select "SYNC" followed by the "START/ STOP" button.
6. When times reach 10 minutes, press "START/ PAUSE" and shake the Ingredients. Reinsert drawers to resume cooking.
7. Bon appétit!

Beef Fried Rice

Serves 6

Prep time: 10 minutes / Cook time: 20 minutes

Ingredients

- 226g Skirt Steak sliced against the grain
- 4 Cups Cold Cooked White Rice
- 340g White Onion Diced
- 21g Celery Diced
- 21g Carrots Diced

- 4-6 Tbsp Soy Sauce or Gluten Free Soy Sauce
- Coconut Oil Cooking Spray or Olive Oil Cooking Spray
- 2 Great Day Farms Hard-Boiled Eggs

Preparation instructions

1. The steak should be cut, then placed in the air fryer basket. Cook for five minutes at 390 degrees.
2. After flipping, cook for a further five minutes.
3. Use foil to line the air fryer basket. To ensure that air may still flow, make sure not to completely cover the basket. Most of the time, I roll it up on the side.
4. Apply coconut oil or olive oil spray on the foil. Place each item in the basket over the foil in the proper sequence.
5. Add a generous layer of coconut oil spray to the top of the mixture after stirring to combine.
6. Cook for five minutes in the air fryer at 390°.
7. Open the container with care and toss the rice and mixture once more, adding more soy sauce or spray if necessary.
8. Add the sliced or chopped hard-boiled eggs by stirring.
9. Cooking time is extended by 3 minutes at 390°. Stir, then plate.

Cheesy Stuffed Peppers

Serves 6

Prep time: 5 minutes / Cook time: 20 minutes

Ingredients

- 6 medium peppers, deveined
- 400g cooked millet, drained
- 200g cooked or canned red kidney beans, drained
- 1 small tomato, chopped
- Sea salt and ground black pepper, to taste

- 100g Swiss cheese, grated

Preparation instructions

1. Insert crisper plates in both drawers. Spray the crisper plates with nonstick cooking oil. Place the peppers in both drawers.
2. Select zone 1 and pair it with "ROAST" at 180°C for 10 minutes. Select "MATCH" to duplicate settings across both zones. Press the "START/STOP" button.
3. In a mixing bowl, thoroughly combine the other Ingredients. Divide the mixture between bell peppers and arrange the peppers in both drawers of your Ninja Foodi.
4. Select zone 1 and pair it with "BAKE" at 190°C for 10 minutes. Select "MATCH" to duplicate settings across both zones. Press the "START/STOP" button.
5. Enjoy!

Meatloaf with Mashed Potatoes

Serves 5

Prep time: 10 minutes / Cook time: 20 minutes

Ingredients

- 250g pork mince
- 250 beef mince
- 1 small egg, well-beaten
- 2 tbsp barbecue sauce
- 2 garlic cloves, minced
- 1 small leek, chopped
- Sea salt and ground black pepper
- 50g fresh breadcrumbs
- 1 tbsp olive oil
- 170ml tomato paste
- 1 tbsp English mustard
- 500g baby potatoes, scrubbed
- 1 tbsp butter, room temperature

Preparation instructions

1. Brush a loaf tin with nonstick cooking oil.
2. In a mixing bowl, thoroughly combine the pork mince, beef mince, egg, barbecue sauce, garlic, leek, salt, pepper, and breadcrumbs. Press the mixture into the prepared loaf tin and brush it with olive oil.
3. Whisk the tomato paste and mustard until well combined; reserve.
4. Add the meatloaf to the zone 1 drawer. Toss baby potatoes with salt and pepper; spray the potatoes with cooking oil and place them in the zone 2 drawer.
5. Select zone 1 and pair it with "BAKE" at 180°C for 20 minutes. Select zone 2 and pair it with "ROAST" at 200°C for about 18 minutes. Select "SYNC" followed by the "START/STOP" button.
6. When zone 1 time reaches 10 minutes, spread the tomato mixture over the top of your meatloaf. Reinsert the drawer to continue cooking. (Cook until the centre of your meatloaf reaches 74°C).
7. Toss baby potatoes to ensure even cooking. Mash baby potatoes with butter and serve immediately.
8. Bon appétit!

Carnitas Enchiladas

Serves 4

Prep time: 10 minutes / Cook time: 1 hour 10 minutes

Ingredients

- 800g pork shoulder, cut into 4 pieces
- 1 tsp olive oil
- Sea salt and ground black pepper, to taste
- 8 small corn tortillas
- Enchilada Sauce:

- 1 tbsp olive oil
- 1 tsp ground cumin
- 1 tsp garlic powder
- 3 tbsp tomato paste
- 200ml chicken broth
- 1 tbsp fresh lime juice
- 1 jalapeño pepper, deveined

Preparation instructions

1. Insert crisper plates in zone 1 and 2 drawers. Spray the crisper plates with nonstick cooking oil.
2. Toss pork shoulder with 1 teaspoon of olive oil, salt, and black pepper. Divide the pork shoulder between both drawers.
3. Select zone 1 and pair it with "ROAST" at 175°C for 55 minutes. Select "MATCH" to duplicate settings across both zones. Press the "START/STOP" button.
4. At the halfway point, gently flip the meat, and reinsert the drawers to resume cooking.
5. Meanwhile, mix all the sauce Ingredients until well combined.
6. Shred the pork with two forks and divide it between tortillas; top with cheese and roll tightly to assemble your enchiladas.
7. Divide enchiladas between two lightly greased baking tins; spoon the sauce over them and add them to both drawers (without crisper plates).
8. Select zone 1 and pair it with "BAKE" at 190°C for 15 minutes, until the edges of the tortillas are slightly browned. Select "MATCH" to duplicate settings across both zones. Press the "START/STOP" button.
9. Bon appétit!

Tuna Jacket Potatoes

Serves 4

Prep time: 10 minutes / Cook time: 35 minutes

Ingredients

- 4 (220g each) russet potatoes
- 2 tsp English mustard
- 1 (185g) can tuna in oil, drained
- 2 spring onions, sliced
- 4 sun-dried tomatoes in oil, chopped
- 6 tbsp sour cream
- 1 small chilli, minced
- Sea salt and ground black pepper, to taste

Preparation instructions

1. Pierce your potatoes with a fork a few times. Place the potatoes in both drawers.
2. Select zone 1 and pair it with "BAKE" at 200°C for 35 minutes. Select "MATCH" to duplicate settings across both zones. Press the "START/STOP" button.
3. Meanwhile, mix the remaining Ingredients for the filling.
4. When zone 1 time reaches 20 minutes, split the potatoes down the middle. Now, divide the filling between your potatoes; reinsert the drawers to continue cooking.
5. Taste, adjust the seasoning and enjoy!

Old-Fashioned Fruit Fritters

Serves 4

Prep time: 5 minutes / Cook time: 10 minutes

Ingredients

- 100g all-purpose flour
- 2 tbsp corn flour
- 1 tsp baking powder
- A pinch of sea salt
- A pinch of grated nutmeg
- 1/2 tsp ground cinnamon
- 1 large egg
- 4 tbsp golden syrup
- 50ml full-fat milk
- 1 tsp vanilla bean paste

- 1 medium pear, cored and chopped
- 1 medium apple, cored and chopped
- 1 tbsp coconut oil

Preparation instructions

1. Line both drawers with parchment paper.
2. In a mixing bowl, thoroughly combine all dry Ingredients.
3. Now, separate the egg yolk from the egg white. Beat the egg yolk with golden syrup, milk, and vanilla until pale and frothy.
4. Beat the egg white until stiff peaks form. Carefully add the egg white to the mixture.
5. Add the liquid Ingredients to the dry Ingredients; fold in the fruit and gently stir until everything is well incorporated.
6. Use a cookie scoop to create the dollops of batter and arrange them in both drawers. Drizzle your fritters with coconut oil.
7. Select zone 1 and pair it with "AIR FRY" at 185°C for 9 to 10 minutes. Select "MATCH" followed by the "START/STOP" button.
8. Dust with icing sugar if desired and serve at room temperature. Enjoy!

Cheeseburger Casserole

Serves 4

Prep time: 5 minutes / Cook time: 40 minutes

Ingredients

- 800g beef mince
- 1 tbsp olive oil
- 100ml chicken stock
- 1 medium ripe tomato, chopped
- 1 tbsp beef bouillon granules
- Sea salt and ground black pepper, to taste
- 1 tsp paprika
- 1 tsp sumac
- 1 small leek, peeled and chopped

- 2 medium bell peppers, deveined and sliced
- 1 medium carrot, cut into bite-sized pieces
- 150g cheddar cheese, grated

Preparation instructions

1. Add all the Ingredients to a large bowl and stir until everything is well combined.
2. Spoon the mixture into two lightly-greased baking tins. Add the baking tins to the drawers (without crisper plates).
3. Select zone 1 and pair it with "ROAST" at 180°C for 40 minutes. Select "MATCH" followed by the "START/STOP" button.
4. At the halfway point, gently stir the Ingredients using a wooden spoon. Reinsert drawers to resume cooking.
5. Bon appétit!

Cheeseburger

Serves 6

Prep time: 3 minutes / Cook time: 12 minutes

Ingredients

- 900g ribeye or New York steak, cut into 1-inch cubes
- 16.8g sea salt
- 8g black pepper
- 8g garlic powder
- 16g onion powder
- 8g paprika
- 16g rosemary crushed
- 16g coconut aminos

Preparation instructions

1. Steak cubes should be placed in a medium bowl.
2. Combine the salt, pepper, paprika, onion, garlic, and rosemary in a small bowl. Mix thoroughly.
3. On the steak cubes, generously sprinkle the

mixed dry spice. To spread the seasoning equally, stir.

4. The steak has been season with the coconut aminos. Mix thoroughly.

5. Give it five minutes to sit.

6. Put the steak in the air fryer basket in a single layer.

7. Cook for 12 minutes at 380F. To ensure that the steak cooks evenly, shake the basket halfway through.

8. Before serving, take it out of the air fryer and let it cool for a while.

Chicken Thighs with Roasted Vegetables

Serves 3

Prep time: 5 minutes / Cook time: 28 minutes

Ingredients

- 3 (200g each) chicken thighs
- 300g baby carrots, sliced
- 300g courgettes, sliced
- 2 tbsp butter, melted
- 1 tbsp fresh lemon juice
- 1/2 tsp dried dill
- 1 tsp paprika
- Kosher salt and ground black pepper, to taste

Preparation instructions

1. Add all the Ingredients to a resealable bag; give it a good shake until chicken thighs and veggies are well coated.

2. Add chicken thighs to the zone 1 drawer and vegetables to the zone 2 drawer.

3. Select zone 1 and pair it with "AIR FRY" at 200°C for 25 to 28 minutes. Select zone 2 and pair it with "ROAST" at 200°C for 16 minutes. Select "SYNC" followed by the "START/STOP" button.

4. When zone 1 time reaches 14 minutes, shake the drawer and reinsert it to continue cooking.

5. When zone 2 time reaches 6 minutes, toss the drawer and reinsert it to continue cooking.

6. Enjoy!

Mexican-Style Taquitos

Serves 4

Prep time: 10 minutes / Cook time: 44 minutes

Ingredients

- 2 tsp olive oil
- 600g chicken fillets
- 1 tsp chilli powder
- Sea salt and freshly ground black pepper, to taste
- 1 medium onion, peeled and sliced
- 1 small garlic clove, pressed
- 100ml salsa verde
- 8 small tortillas

Preparation instructions

1. Insert crisper plates in both drawers. Spray the crisper plates with nonstick cooking oil.

2. Toss chicken fillets with 1 tsp of olive oil and spices. Divide the chicken fillets between the zone 1 and zone 2 drawers.

3. Select zone 1 and pair it with "AIR FRY" at 190°C for 34 minutes. Select "MATCH" to duplicate settings across both zones. Press the "START/STOP" button.

4. Flip the chicken fillets once or twice to promote even cooking. Then, cut the chicken into strips and add the onion, garlic, salsa, salt, and pepper.

5. Divide the chicken filling between small tortillas. Roll them up and arrange your taquitos on both crisper plates.

6. Select zone 1 and pair it with "BAKE" at

180°C for 10 minutes. Select "MATCH" to duplicate settings across both zones. Press the "START/STOP" button.

7. Enjoy!

Fish and Chips

Serves 2

Prep time: 10 minutes / Cook time: 24 minutes

Ingredients

- 2 (170g each) skinned tilapia fillet (or white fish of choice)
- 1 tsp chilli flakes
- 1 garlic clove, peeled
- 1 tsp dried rosemary leaves
- 1 small egg, beaten
- Sea salt and ground black pepper, to taste
- 60g plain flour
- 50g dried breadcrumbs
- 450g potato, peeled, thin hand-cut chips (Maris Piper, King Edward, or Russet potatoes).
- 2 tsp olive oil

Preparation instructions

1. Pat tilapia fillets dry using tea towels. Crush the chilli flakes, garlic, and rosemary leaves using a pestle and mortar; reserve.
2. Now, make the breading station: Beat the egg until pale and frothy. In a separate shallow dish, mix the salt, pepper, and flour. In a third shallow dish, thoroughly combine the breadcrumbs with the spice mixture.
3. Dust fish fillets with the flour mixture, and then, dip them in the egg. Roll them over the breadcrumb mixture. Arrange the prepared fish fillets on the crisper plate and spray them with 1 teaspoon of oil.
4. Toss potato chips with salt, black pepper, and

1 teaspoon of olive oil.

5. Select zone 1 and pair it with "AIR FRY" at 200°C for 14 minutes. Select zone 2 and pair it with "AIR FRY" at 200°C for 24 minutes. Select "SYNC" followed by the "START/STOP" button.
6. When zone 1 time reaches 9 minutes, turn the fish fillets over using silicone-tipped tongs and spray them with cooking oil on the other side. Reinsert the drawer to continue cooking.
7. When zone 2 time reaches 12 minutes, shake the drawer for a few seconds to promote even cooking. Reinsert the drawer to continue cooking.
8. Bon appétit!

Air Fryer Ham

Serves 4

Prep time: 5 minutes / Cook time: 50 minutes

Ingredients

- 1.2 Kg Ham/Gammon Joint
- 6 Tbsp Honey
- 4 Tbsp Heinz Mustard
- 2 Tbsp Garlic Puree

Preparation instructions

1. Use a sharp knife to trim the ham of its fat. Make cube-like scores on the ham joint.
2. Honey, garlic, and mustard should all be well combined in a bowl after being properly mixed, put a thick layer of marinade on the ham, being sure to get it into the scored areas.
3. Put the ham on the rod skewers, then cook it in your Ninja foodi air fryer. Cook for a further 25 minutes at 170 °C after 25 minutes at 200 °C .
4. Slice your ham after taking off the rod.

French onion tarts

Serves 2

Prep time: 10 minutes / Cook time: 30 minutes

Ingredients
- 2 sheets shortcrust pastry, just thawed
- 1 tbsp olive oil
- 1 small brown onion, thinly sliced
- 75g cream cheese
- 2 tbsp sour cream
- 25g grated cheddar
- 3 large eggs
- Chopped fresh chives, to serve (optional)

Preparation instructions
1. Lightly grease two 11.5cm fluted tartlet tins.
2. One pastry sheet should be placed on a gently dusted work surface. Add the last pastry layer on top. Add a little flour, then roll out to a thickness of 3 mm. Cut diagonally in half. In one prepared tart tin, gently place one half. Repeat with the remaining tart tin and pastry half. Trim any extra pastry. Fill the pastry casings with rice or pastry weights after lining them with parchment paper. Put the food in the basket of airfryer and fry for 6 minutes at 200C. Remove the paper and rice or beans, air fry for a further two minutes.
3. Meanwhile, heat the oil in a frying pan over medium heat. Add onion and cook, stirring occasionally, for 10 minutes or until golden and caramelised. Set aside to cool slightly.
4. Combine cream cheese , sour cream , cheddar and 1 egg in a bowl. Add the onion. Stir to combine. Season. Divide the mixture between tart cases. Make a small well in the centre of 1 tart. Crack an egg into the well. Repeat with remaining tart and egg. Season with pepper.
5. Air fry at 170°C for 10-12 minutes or until just cooked. Leave in the air fryer to cool for 5 minutes or until the egg is cooked to your liking. Sprinkle with chives , if using, to serve.

Chicken with Cheesy Brussels Sprouts

Serves 4

Prep time: 10 minutes / Cook time: 33 minutes

Ingredients
- 600g chicken breasts, boneless, skinless, cut into 4 pieces
- 600g Brussels sprouts, halved
- 2 tsp olive oil
- 1/2 tsp garlic granules
- Sea salt and ground black pepper, to taste
- 1 tsp paprika
- 100g parmesan cheese, grated

Preparation instructions
1. Insert crisper plate in both drawers. Spray the crisper plates with nonstick cooking oil. Toss chicken breasts and Brussels sprouts with olive oil, garlic granules, salt, black pepper, and paprika.
2. Place the chicken breasts in the zone 1 drawer and the Brussels sprouts in the zone 2 drawer.
3. Select zone 1 and pair it with "AIR FRY" at 190°C for 33 minutes. Select zone 2 and pair it with "AIR FRY" at 200°C for 18 minutes. Select "SYNC" followed by the "START/ STOP" button.
4. At the halfway point, flip the Ingredients with silicone-tipped tongs to promote even cooking. Toss Brussels sprouts with cheese and reinsert drawers to resume cooking.
5. Bon appétit!

CHAPTER 4 POULTRY

Chicken Wings with Glazed Vegetables

Serves 4

Prep time: 5 minutes / Cook time: 28 minutes

Ingredients
- 600g chicken wings
- 300g carrots, sliced
- 300g parsnip, sliced
- 2 tbsp butter, melted
- 1 tbsp honey
- 1 (1 cm) knob ginger, peeled and grated
- 1 tbsp orange juice
- Kosher salt and ground black pepper, to taste

Preparation instructions
1. Add all the Ingredients to a resealable bag; give it a good shake until chicken thighs and carrots are well coated on all sides.
2. Add chicken thighs to the zone 1 drawer and vegetables to the zone 2 drawer.
3. Select zone 1 and pair it with "AIR FRY" at 200°C for 25 to 28 minutes. Select zone 2 and pair it with "ROAST" at 190°C for 16 minutes. Select "SYNC" followed by the "START/STOP" button.
4. When zone 1 time reaches 14 minutes, shake the drawer and reinsert it to continue cooking.
5. When zone 2 time reaches 8 minutes, turn the carrots over and reinsert the drawer to continue cooking.
6. Enjoy!

Turkey Thights with Roast Potatoes

Serves 4

Prep time: 5 minutes / Cook time: 40 minutes

Ingredients
- 500g turkey thighs
- 1 tsp dried sage
- 1 tsp onion granules
- 1 tsp garlic granules
- 1 tsp chilli flakes, crushed
- 1 tbsp olive oil
- 500g Russet potatoes, peeled and cut into 2.5cm wedges

Preparation instructions
1. Add all the Ingredients to a resealable bag; give it a good shake until turkey thighs and potatoes are well coated on all sides.
2. Add turkey thighs to the zone 1 drawer and potatoes to the zone 2 drawer.
3. Select zone 1 and pair it with "AIR FRY" at 175°C for 40 minutes. Select zone 2 and pair it with "ROAST" at 200°C for 20 minutes. Select "SYNC" followed by the "START/STOP" button.
4. When zone 1 time reaches 20 minutes, shake the drawer and reinsert it to continue cooking.
5. When zone 2 time reaches 10 minutes, shake the drawer and reinsert it to continue cooking.
6. Enjoy!

Crusted Chicken Tenders air fryer

Serves 4

Prep time: 15 minutes / Cook time: 15 minutes

Ingredients

- 3 tablespoons all-purpose flour
- ¼ teaspoon ground turmeric
- ¼ teaspoon freshly ground black pepper
- ¼ teaspoon mustard powder
- 3 ½ ounces salted pretzels, crushed
- 1 large egg, beaten
- 680g chicken tenderloins
- olive oil cooking spray

Preparation instructions

1. Set the Ninja Foodi air fryer at 400 degrees Fahrenheit (200 degrees C).
2. Combine the flour, mustard powder, turmeric, black pepper, and it in a large zip-top plastic bag. Shake the bag after sealing it after completely combining the dry Ingredients.
3. On one plate, scatter the crushed pretzels. On a another plate, place the parchment paper. Add the chicken tenders to the bag of seasoned flour after patting them dry with paper towels. After shaking the tenders to coat them lightly, reseal the bag.
4. With your clean non-dominant hand, throw pretzels onto the top of each tender after dipping it into the egg and brushing off the excess. Put a few pretzels that have been crushed inside each tender.
5. Each pretzel-coated tender should be placed on the parchment-lined dish. On both sides, apply cooking spray with olive oil.
6. In the air fryer that has been preheated, arrange the chicken tenders in a single layer.

For 6 minutes, air fry. After 5 to 6 minutes of air frying, the chicken shouldn't be pink at the bone and the fluids should run clear. Using tongs, gently rotate the tenders.

Turkey Burgers

Serves 6

Prep time: 5 minutes / Cook time: 20 minutes

Ingredients

- 800g turkey mince
- 1 medium onion, chopped
- 2 garlic cloves, minced
- 50g seasoned breadcrumbs
- Sea salt and ground black pepper, to taste
- 1/2 tsp smoked paprika
- 5 burger buns
- 150g cherry tomatoes, halved
- 8 Romaine lettuce
- 1 tbsp English mustard

Preparation instructions

1. Insert a crisper plate in each drawer. Spray the crisper plates with nonstick cooking oil.
2. Thoroughly combine the turkey mince, onion, garlic, breadcrumbs, and spices. Shape the mixture into six patties and spray them with cooking oil.
3. Add burgers to each drawer and spray them with cooking oil.
4. Select zone 1 and pair it with "AIR FRY" at 190°C for 20 minutes. Select "MATCH" to duplicate settings across both zones. Press the "START/STOP" button.
5. When zone 1 time reaches 10 minutes, turn the burgers over and spray them with cooking oil on the other side. Reinsert the drawer to continue cooking.
6. Serve your burgers in the buns topped with

tomatoes, lettuce, and mustard.

7. Bon appétit!

Turkey Satay Salad

Serves 6

Prep time: 5 minutes / Cook time: 55 minutes

Ingredients

- Salad:
- 500g turkey breast fillets
- 1 tsp olive oil
- 200g carrots, peeled, cut into 1.5cm pieces
- 200g asparagus, trimmed
- 2 medium Gem lettuce hearts, cut into wedges
- 1 small onion, thinly sliced
- Dressing:
- 1 tbsp peanut oil
- 2 tbsp fresh lemon juice
- 1 tbsp soy sauce
- 1/2 tsp mustard seeds
- 1 tsp ginger-garlic paste
- 1 tsp agave syrup
- 1 tbsp peanut butter

Preparation instructions

1. Insert a crisper plate in each drawer. Spray the crisper plates with nonstick cooking oil.
2. Toss turkey, carrots, and asparagus with olive oil.
3. Place turkey breast fillets in the zone 1 drawer and carrots with asparagus in the zone 2 drawer.
4. Select zone 1 and pair it with "AIR FRY" at 175°C for 55 minutes. Select zone 2 and pair it with "ROAST" at 200°C for 15 minutes. Select "SYNC" followed by the "START/ STOP" button.
5. Turn the turkey breast fillets 2- 3 times

during the cooking time to ensure even browning. Shake the drawer with veggies halfway through the cooking time.

6. Meanwhile, add lettuce and onion to a salad bowl. Whisk all the dressing Ingredients.
7. Add turkey, carrots, and asparagus to a salad bowl and toss to combine.
8. Enjoy!

Blackened Chicken Breast

Serves 3

Prep time: 15 minutes / Cook time: 15 minutes

Ingredients

- 2 tsp paprika
- 1 tsp ground thyme
- 1 tsp cumin
- ½ tsp cayenne pepper
- ½ tsp onion powder
- ½ tsp black pepper
- ¼ tsp salt
- 2 tsp vegetable oil
- 2 (340g) skinless, boneless chicken breast halves

Preparation instructions

1. In a mixing bowl, combine the paprika, thyme, cumin, cayenne pepper, onion powder, black pepper, and salt. Place spice mixture on a flat dish.
2. Coat each chicken breast with oil. Roll each piece of chicken in the blackening spice mixture, pressing down to ensure the spice adheres to all sides. Allow it rest for 5 minutes while you warm the air fryer.
3. Preheat an air fryer to 360°F (175°C) for 5 minutes.
4. Cook the chicken for 10 minutes in the air fryer basket. Cook for an additional 10

minutes on the other side. Transfer the chicken to a platter and set aside for 5 minutes before serving.

Chicken Kievs

Serves 6

Prep time: 5 minutes / Cook time: 34 minutes

Ingredients

- 6 (150-175g each) chicken breasts, skinless and boneless
- 1 tbsp olive oil
- 1 tsp hot paprika
- Sea salt and ground black pepper, to taste
- 80g dried breadcrumbs
- 80g parmesan, grated

Preparation instructions

1. Rub the chicken with olive oil, paprika, salt, and black pepper. Then, roll the chicken over the breadcrumbs.
2. Insert crisper plates in both drawers. Spray the crisper plates with nonstick cooking oil.
3. Place the chicken breasts in both drawers.
4. Select zone 1 and pair it with "AIR FRY" at 190°C for 34 minutes. Select "MATCH" to duplicate settings across both zones. Press the "START/STOP" button.
5. At the halfway point, flip the chicken breasts with silicone-tipped tongs and top them with parmesan cheese. Reinsert drawers to resume cooking.
6. Enjoy!

Frozen Chicken Nuggets with Broccoli

Serves 4

Prep time: 5 minutes / Cook time: 10 minutes

Ingredients

- 400g frozen chicken nuggets
- 500g broccoli, cut into 2.5cm florets
- 20g Dijon mustard
- 40g mayonnaise
- 1 tbsp honey
- 1/2 tsp garlic granules
- Sea salt and ground black pepper, to taste

Preparation instructions

1. Insert crisper plates in both drawers. Spray the crisper plates with nonstick cooking oil.
2. Spray chicken nuggets with nonstick cooking oil. Toss broccoli florets with mustard, mayo, honey, garlic, salt, and black pepper.
3. Place the chicken nuggets in the zone 1 drawer and the broccoli florets in the zone 2 drawer.
4. Select zone 1 and pair it with "MAX CRISP" for 10 minutes. Select zone 2 and pair it with "ROAST" at 200°C for 9 minutes. Select "SYNC" followed by the "START/STOP" button.
5. Shake the drawers halfway through the cooking time to promote even cooking.
6. Bon appétit!

Duck Traybake

Serves 4

Prep time: 5 minutes / Cook time: 30 minutes

Ingredients

- 800 g duck legs
- 300ml tomato purée
- 1 tbsp soy sauce
- 1 tbsp stone-ground mustard
- Sea salt and ground black pepper, to taste
- 2 thyme sprigs
- 1 rosemary sprig
- 1 tsp olive oil
- 1 medium pepper, sliced
- 1 medium courgette, sliced
- 2 cloves garlic, smashed

Preparation instructions

1. Remove a crisper plate from your Ninja Foodi. Brush two baking tins with nonstick oil.
2. Divide the Ingredients between two baking tins.
3. Select zone 1 and pair it with "AIR FRY" at 170°C for 15 minutes. Select "MATCH" to duplicate settings across both zones. Press the "START/STOP" button.
4. At the halfway point, increase the temperature to 200°C; continue to cook for a further 15 minutes.
5. Enjoy!

Chicken Fajitas

Serves 4

Prep time: 10 minutes / Cook time: 40 minutes

Ingredients

- 4 chicken breasts (200g each), skinless, boneless, cut into strips
- 2 large onions, peeled and sliced
- 2 large bell peppers, deseeded and sliced
- 2 tbsp olive oil
- 1 tsp garlic powder
- 1 tsp Mexican oregano
- Sea salt and freshly ground black pepper, to taste
- 1 medium tomato, chopped
- 1 red chilli pepper, deveined and minced
- 4 large tortillas

Preparation instructions

1. Insert crisper plates in both drawers. Spray the crisper plates with nonstick cooking oil.
2. Toss chicken breasts, onion, and bell peppers with olive oil and seasoning.
3. Place the turkey breasts in the zone 1 drawer and the vegetables in the zone 2 drawer.
4. Select zone 1 and pair it with "AIR FRY" at 175°C for 40 minutes. Select zone 2 and pair it with "ROAST" at 200°C for 16 minutes. Select "SYNC" followed by the "START/ STOP" button.
5. Flip the Ingredients once or twice to promote even cooking. Reinsert drawers to resume cooking.
6. Add the turkey strips to the warmed tortillas; top them with roasted veggies, tomato, and chilli pepper. Roll them up and enjoy!

Herb Chicken with Asparagus

Serves 4

Prep time: 5 minutes / Cook time: 25 minutes

Ingredients

- 600g frozen chicken tenders
- 2 tbsp olive oil
- 1 tbsp dried oregano
- 1 tsp dried basil
- 1 tbsp dried rosemary
- 1 garlic clove, pressed
- Sea salt and ground black pepper, to taste
- 1/2 tsp hot paprika
- 600g asparagus, trimmed

Preparation instructions

1. Insert crisper plates in both drawers.
2. Toss chicken tenders and asparagus with the oil and spices.
3. Spray the crisper plates with nonstick cooking oil. Place the chicken tenders in the zone 1 drawer and the asparagus in the zone 2 drawer.
4. Select zone 1 and pair it with "AIR FRY" at 190°C for 25 minutes. Select zone 2 and pair it with "AIR FRY" at 200°C for 16 minutes. Select "SYNC" followed by the "START/STOP" button.
5. When times reach 12 minutes, press "START/PAUSE" and shake the Ingredients. Reinsert drawers to resume cooking.
6. Taste and adjust the seasonings. Serve warm chicken with asparagus on the side.
7. Bon appétit!

Air Fryer Chicken Parmesan

Serves 4-6

Prep time: 10 minutes / Cook time: 15-20 minutes

Ingredients

- 4 boneless, skinless chicken breasts (600g)
- 60g Italian seasoned breadcrumbs
- 30g grated Parmesan cheese
- 30g all-purpose flour
- 1 egg, beaten
- 240ml marinara sauce
- 120g shredded mozzarella cheese
- Salt and pepper, to taste
- Cooking spray

Preparation instructions

1. Preheat the air fryer to 200°C.
2. Season the chicken breasts with salt and pepper.
3. In a shallow bowl, mix together the breadcrumbs and grated Parmesan cheese.
4. In another shallow bowl, add the flour.
5. In a third shallow bowl, beat the egg.
6. Dip each chicken breast in the flour, then the egg, and then the breadcrumb mixture, making sure it is well coated.
7. Spray the air fryer basket with cooking spray.
8. Place the chicken breasts in the air fryer basket, making sure they are not touching.
9. Cook for 10 minutes, then flip the chicken breasts and cook for another 5-10 minutes, or until the chicken is cooked through and the coating is crispy.
10. Spoon marinara sauce over each chicken breast, then sprinkle with shredded mozzarella cheese.
11. Cook in the air fryer for an additional 2-3 minutes, or until the cheese is melted and bubbly. Serve hot, with a side of pasta or vegetables if desired. Enjoy!

Roast Turkey Breast

Serves 4

Prep time: 5 minutes / Cook time: 1 hour

Ingredients

- 1 kg turkey breasts, skin-on, boneless, cut into two pieces
- 2 tsp olive oil
- 2 tbsp Dijon mustard
- 1 tsp onion powder
- 1 tsp garlic powder
- 1 tsp paprika

Preparation instructions

1. Insert crisper plates in both drawers. Spray the crisper plates with nonstick cooking oil.
2. Pat turkey breasts dry with paper towels. Rub the olive oil, mustard, and spices over the skin using your hands to coat everything in the spice mixture. Transfer the turkey breasts to the zone 1 ad 2 drawers.
3. Select zone 1 and pair it with "ROAST" at 200°C for 1 hour. Select "MATCH" to duplicate settings across both zones. Press the "START/STOP" button.
4. At the halfway point, turn the turkey breasts over and reinsert the drawers to resume cooking.
5. Bon appétit!

Mini Meatloaf Cups

Serves 6

Prep time: 10 minutes / Cook time: 20 minutes

Ingredients

- 600g turkey mince
- 50g bacon lardons
- 1 medium egg, well-beaten
- 1 medium onion, chopped
- 2 garlic cloves, minced
- 1 large bell pepper, seeded and chopped
- 120g fresh breadcrumbs
- 170ml tomato paste
- 1 tbsp dried mustard
- 1 tsp honey (or golden syrup)

Preparation instructions

1. Brush 6 muffin cases with nonstick cooking oil.
2. Mix the turkey mince, bacon, egg, onion, garlic, bell pepper, and breadcrumbs until everything is well incorporated.
3. Mix the tomato paste with mustard and honey; reserve.
4. Press the turkey mince mixture into the prepared muffin cases. Place them in both drawers.
5. Select zone 1 and pair it with "AIR FRY" at 180°C for 20 minutes. Select "MATCH" to duplicate settings across both zones. Press the "START/STOP" button.
6. When zone 1 time reaches 10 minutes, spread the tomato mixture over the meatloaf cups and bake for a further 10 minutes, until the centre of your meatloaf reaches 74°C. Reinsert the drawers to continue cooking.
7. Bon appétit!

Chicken Drumettes with Fine Green Beans

Serves 5

Prep time: 5 minutes / Cook time: 33 minutes

Ingredients

- 600g chicken drumettes
- 2 tbsp butter, melted
- 1 tsp ginger-garlic paste
- 1 tbsp soy sauce
- Kosher salt and ground black pepper, to taste
- 500g fine green beans, trimmed

Preparation instructions

1. Add all the Ingredients to a resealable bag; give it a good shake until chicken drumettes and green beans are well coated on all sides.
2. Add chicken drumettes to the zone 1 drawer and green beans to the zone 2 drawer.
3. Select zone 1 and pair it with "AIR FRY" at 200°C for 33 minutes. Select zone 2 and pair it with "AIR FRY" at 200°C for 16 minutes. Select "SYNC" followed by the "START/ STOP" button.
4. When zone 1 time reaches 16 minutes, shake the drawer and reinsert it to continue cooking.
5. When zone 2 time reaches 8 minutes, turn the green beans over and reinsert the drawer to continue cooking.
6. Enjoy!

Chicken Nuggets from Scratch

Serves 5

Prep time: 10 minutes + marinating time / Cook time: 18 minutes

Ingredients

- 600g chicken, boneless, skinless
- 1 tbsp English mustard
- 150 ml plain yoghurt
- 1/2 tsp garlic granules
- Sea salt and ground black pepper, to taste
- 120g fresh breadcrumbs, crushed
- 1 tbsp olive oil

Preparation instructions

1. Insert crisper plates in both drawers. Spray the crisper plates with nonstick cooking oil.
2. Cut the chicken into bite-sized pieces; then, place the chicken pieces in a ceramic (glass) bowl; add mustard and yoghurt, and let it marinate in your fridge for about 2 hours.
3. Discard the marinade and season the chicken pieces with garlic granules, salt, and black pepper.
4. Place the breadcrumbs on a plate and then, roll each chicken piece onto the breadcrumbs, pressing to adhere. Brush the chicken pieces with olive oil on all sides.
5. Divide the chicken pieces between both drawers.
6. Select zone 1 and pair it with "AIR FRY" at 200°C for 18 minutes. Select "MATCH" to duplicate settings across both zones. Press the "START/STOP" button.
7. At the halfway point, toss the drawer to ensure even cooking. Enjoy!

Turkey Ragù with Rosemary Potatoes

Serves 5

Prep time: 5 minutes / Cook time: 25 minutes

Ingredients
- 500g turkey mince
- 2 tsp olive oil
- 1 large carrot, grated
- 1 large onion, chopped
- 2 cloves garlic, finely diced
- 1 tbsp Marmite
- 2 medium tins of tomatoes, crushed
- 500g potatoes, peeled and cut into wedges
- 2 rosemary sprigs, leaves picked and crushed
- Sea salt and ground black pepper, to your liking

Preparation instructions
1. In a mixing bowl, place turkey mince, 1 tsp of olive oil, carrot, onion, garlic, Marmite and tomatoes; gently stir to combine. Spoon the veg/turkey mixture into a baking tin.
2. Toss potato wedges with rosemary, salt, black pepper, and the remaining 1 teaspoon of olive oil.
3. Add the baking tin to the zone 1 drawer and the potatoes to the zone 2 drawer (with the crisper plate).
4. Select zone 1 and pair it with "BAKE" at 180°C for 25 minutes. Select zone 2 and pair it with "AIR FRY" at 180°C for 20 minutes. Select "SYNC" followed by the "START/STOP" button.
5. When zone 1 time reaches 12 minutes, gently stir the Ingredients and reinsert it to continue cooking.
6. When zone 2 time reaches 10 minutes, toss the drawer and reinsert it to continue cooking.
7. Enjoy!

Chicken Spiedie

Serves 4-6

Prep time: 30 minutes (including marinade time) / Cook time: 10-12 minutes

Ingredients
- 680g boneless, skinless chicken breasts, cut into 2.5cm cubes
- 60ml olive oil
- 60ml red wine vinegar
- 60ml lemon juice
- 15g chopped fresh parsley
- 1 tablespoon dried oregano
- 1 tablespoon minced garlic
- Salt and pepper, to taste
- 4-6 skewers

Preparation instructions
1. In a large bowl, whisk together the olive oil, red wine vinegar, lemon juice, parsley, oregano, and garlic.
2. Season the chicken cubes with salt and pepper, then add them to the bowl with the marinade.
3. Toss the chicken in the marinade until well coated.
4. Cover the bowl with plastic wrap and marinate in the refrigerator for at least 2 hours (or overnight for best flavor).
5. When ready to cook, preheat the air fryer to 200°C.
6. Thread the chicken cubes onto the skewers.
7. Spray the air fryer basket with cooking spray, then place the chicken skewers in the basket.
8. Cook for 5-6 minutes on each side, or until the chicken is cooked through and slightly charred.
9. Serve hot with a side of salad, vegetables, or bread. Enjoy!

Air Fryer Turkey Burgers

Serves 4

Prep time: 10 minutes / Cook time: 12-15 minutes

Ingredients

- 450g ground turkey
- 30g seasoned breadcrumbs
- 30g grated Parmesan cheese
- 30g chopped fresh parsley
- 1 egg, beaten
- 2 cloves garlic, minced
- Salt and pepper, to taste
- 4 hamburger buns
- Lettuce, tomato, onion, and other desired toppings
- Cooking spray

Preparation instructions

1. Preheat the air fryer to 190°C.
2. In a large bowl, mix together the ground turkey, breadcrumbs, Parmesan cheese, parsley, egg, garlic, salt, and pepper until well combined.
3. Form the mixture into 4 patties.
4. Spray the air fryer basket with cooking spray.
5. Place the turkey burgers in the air fryer basket, making sure they are not touching.
6. Cook for 6-7 minutes, then flip the burgers and cook for another 5-6 minutes, or 7.until the burgers are cooked through and reach an internal temperature of 74°C.
8. Toast the hamburger buns in the air fryer for 1-2 minutes.
9. Assemble the burgers with the buns, lettuce, tomato, onion, and any other desired toppings.
10. Serve hot and enjoy!

Chicken Souvlaki

Serves 5

Prep time: 5 minutes / Cook time: 25 minutes

Ingredients

- 800g chicken breasts, boneless, cut into bite-sized pieces
- Sea salt and ground black pepper, to taste
- 1 tsp garlic granules
- 1 lemon, freshly squeezed
- 1 tsp brown mustard
- 1 tbsp olive oil
- 4 bamboo skewers (soaked in water for 30 minutes)
- 4 large pitta wraps
- 4 tbsp Greek-style tzatziki

Preparation instructions

1. Insert crisper plates in both drawers. Spray the crisper plates with nonstick cooking oil.
2. Toss the chicken breasts with spices, lemon juice, mustard, and olive oil.
3. Thread the chicken pieces onto the soaked bamboo skewers; now, arrange the skewers in both drawers.
4. Select zone 1 and pair it with "AIR FRY" at 180°C for 25 minutes. Select "MATCH" to duplicate settings across both zones. Press the "START/STOP" button.
5. Serve chicken souvlaki with pita and tzatziki.
6. Enjoy!

CHAPTER 5 FISH & SEAFOOD

Old Bay Cod Fish

Serves 4

Prep time: 10 minutes / Cook time: 18 minutes

Ingredients

- 6 (150g each) cod fillets
- 2 small eggs, beaten
- Sea salt and ground black pepper, to taste
- 1 tsp garlic granules
- 1 tsp onion powder
- 150g plain flour
- 150g tortilla chips, crushed
- 1 tbsp Old Bay seasoning

Preparation instructions

1. Insert crisper plates in both drawers. Spray crisper plates with nonstick cooking oil. Pat the cod fish fillets dry with paper towels.
2. Create the breading station: Beat the egg until pale and frothy. In a separate shallow dish, mix the salt, pepper, garlic granules, onion, powder, and flour. In a third dish, thoroughly combine the crushed tortilla chips with Old Bay seasoning
3. Now, use your hands to coat the fish in the flour. Dip codfish fillets in the beaten eggs; roll them over the breadcrumb mixture.
4. Arrange the prepared fish fillets on the lightly greased crisper plates.
5. Select zone 1 and pair it with "AIR FRY" at 180°C for 18 minutes. Select "MATCH" to duplicate settings across both zones. Press the "START/STOP" button.
6. When zone 1 time reaches 9 minutes, turn the fish fillets over to ensure even cooking. Reinsert the drawer to continue cooking.
7. Bon appétit!

Greek-Style Roast Fish

Serves 5

Prep time: 10 minutes / Cook time: 13 minutes

Ingredients

- 5 (150-170g each) tilapia fillets
- 1 tbsp dried sage
- 1 tbsp dried thyme
- 1 tbsp dried parsley
- 2 garlic cloves, peeled
- Sea salt and ground black pepper, to taste
- 2 large tomatoes, cut into slices
- 1 red bell pepper, deveined and sliced
- 2 tsp olive oil
- 1 large lemon, freshly squeezed

Preparation instructions

1. Pat tilapia fillets dry using paper towels. Crush the sage, thyme, parsley, and garlic in a pestle and mortar; reserve.
2. Coat fish fillets with crushed herbs, salt, and pepper; arrange them in two roasting tins, along with tomatoes and bell pepper; drizzle them with olive oil.
3. Add roasting tins to both drawers (without crisper plates).
4. Select zone 1 and pair it with "AIR FRY" at 200°C for 13 minutes. Select "MATCH" to duplicate settings across both zones. Press the "START/STOP" button.
5. When zone 1 time reaches 5 minutes, turn the fish fillets over to ensure even cooking. Reinsert the drawer to continue cooking.
6. When zone 1 time reaches 10 minutes, top the fish fillets with lemon slices and reinsert the drawer to continue cooking.

7. Serve with some extra herbs scattered over and enjoy!

Restaurant-Style Fish & Chips

Serves 3

Prep time: 10 minutes / Cook time: 25 minutes

Ingredients

- 3 (150-160g each) haddock fillets
- 1/2 tsp chilli flakes
- 1/2 tsp garlic granules
- Sea salt and ground black pepper, to taste
- 1 medium egg, beaten
- 80g plain flour
- 80g crushed crackers
- 2 tsp olive oil
- 500g potato, peeled, hand-cut, thick chips (Maris Piper, King Edward, or Russet potatoes)

Preparation instructions

1. Pat fish fillets dry using paper towels; then, coat the fish fillets in spices, using your hands.
2. Now, create the breading station: Beat the egg until frothy. Add the flour to a separate shallow bowl. In a third shallow bowl, place crushed crackers.
3. Dust fish fillets with the flour. Dip fish fillets in the egg, and then, roll them over the crushed crackers. Arrange the prepared fish fillets on the crisper plate in the zone 1 drawer; brush them with 1 teaspoon of olive oil.
4. Toss potato chips with salt, black pepper, and 1 teaspoon of olive oil. Add potato chips to the zone 2 drawer.
5. Select zone 1 and pair it with "AIR FRY" at 180°C for 18 minutes. Select zone 2 and pair it with "AIR FRY" at 200°C for 25 minutes. Select "SYNC" followed by the "START/ STOP" button.

6. When zone 1 time reaches 9 minutes, turn the fish fillets over using silicone-tipped tongs and reinsert the drawer to continue cooking.
7. When zone 2 time reaches 12 minutes, shake the drawer for a few seconds and reinsert
8. Bon appétit!

Salmon Parcels

Serves 4

Prep time: 10 minutes / Cook time: 15 minutes

Ingredients

- 2 tsp olive oil
- 2 garlic cloves, chopped
- 600g cauliflower florets
- 3 spring onions, chopped
- 6 (100-120g each) salmon fillets
- 2 tbsp soy sauce

Preparation instructions

1. Insert crisper plates in both drawers.
2. Now, cut out 6 squares of foil, using scissors (each about 30cm). Brush pieces of foil with olive oil.
3. Divide garlic, cauliflower, and onions between foil pieces. Top them with salmon fillets and drizzle everything with soy sauce.
4. Then, fold over the edges of the foil to seal. Lay the salmon parcels onto the crisper plates.
5. Select zone 1 and pair it with "AIR FRY" at 200°C for 15 minutes. Select "MATCH" to duplicate settings across both zones. Press the "START/STOP" button.
6. When zone 1 time reaches 8 minutes, open the foil. Reinsert the drawer to continue cooking.
7. Bon appétit!

Teriyaki Roast Fish

Serves 4

Prep time: 10 minutes / Cook time: 17 minutes

Ingredients

- 2 tbsp soy sauce
- 1 (about 1 cm-long) knob of fresh ginger, grated
- 2 tbsp mirin
- 2 tsp clear honey
- 2 tsp sesame oil (or olive oil)
- 1 tsp garlic granules
- 4 (170-200g each) halibut steaks

Preparation instructions

1. Mix the soy sauce, freshly grated ginger, mirin, honey, sesame oil, and garlic granules in a small dish.
2. Drizzle the halibut steaks with the sauce and place them in both zones (with crisper plates).
3. Select zone 1 and pair it with "AIR FRY" at 190°C for 17 minutes. Select "MATCH" to duplicate settings across both zones. Press the "START/STOP" button.
4. When zone 1 time reaches 8 minutes, turn the steaks over to ensure even cooking. Reinsert the drawer to continue cooking.
5. Taste and adjust the seasonings. Bon appétit!

Salmon Jerky

Serves 4

Prep time: 10 minutes / Cook time: 3-5 hours

Ingredients

- 1 kg salmon fillet, skin-on, boneless, cut into strips
- 100ml soy sauce
- 1 tbsp lemon juice, freshly squeezed
- 1 tbsp maple syrup
- 100g sea salt
- 2 tsp liquid smoke

Preparation instructions

1. Toss salmon strips with the other Ingredients.
2. Place a single layer of the salmon strips in the drawer. Then add the crisper plate to the drawer on top of the Ingredients; arrange another layer of the salmon strips on the crisper plate.
3. Select zone 1 and pair it with "DEHYDRATE" at 70°C for 3 to 5 hours. Select "MATCH" followed by the "START/STOP" button.
4. Bon appétit!

Cajun Shrimp with Roasted Leeks

Serves 4

Prep time: 10 minutes / Cook time: 12 minutes

Ingredients
- 500g large shrimp, peeled and deveined
- 1 tbsp Cajun spice mix
- 200ml buttermilk
- 150g cornmeal
- 400g leeks, sliced lengthwise

Preparation instructions
1. Insert crisper plates in both drawers and spray them with cooking oil. Pat the shrimp dry using paper towels.
2. Thoroughly combine the Cajun spice mix and buttermilk in a shallow bowl. In a separate shallow bowl, place the cornmeal.
3. Dip your shrimp in the Cajun/buttermilk mixture; now, roll them over the cornmeal. Add the coated shrimp to the zone 1 drawer and the leeks to the zone 2 drawer.
4. Select zone 1 and pair it with "AIR FRY" at 200°C for 10 minutes. Select zone 2 and pair it with "AIR FRY" at 180°C for 12 minutes. Select "SYNC" followed by the "START/ STOP" button.
5. When zone 1 time reaches 5 minutes, shake the drawer and reinsert it to continue cooking.
6. When zone 2 time reaches 6 minutes, shake the drawer for a few seconds and reinsert it to continue cooking.
7. Bon appétit!

Fish Fingers with Cauliflower Mash

Serves 4

Prep time: 10 minutes / Cook time: 20 minutes

Ingredients
- 300g cod fish, skinless
- 50g mayonnaise
- 60 g seasoned breadcrumbs
- 500g cauliflower florets
- Sea salt and ground black pepper, to taste
- 1/2 tsp celery seeds (optional)
- 1 tbsp butter, room temperature
- 1 scallion stalk, chopped

Preparation instructions
1. Insert crisper plates in both drawers and spray them with cooking oil. Pat the fish dry using tea towels. Next, cut the fish into equal strips.
2. Add the mayo to a shallow bowl. Tip the breadcrumbs into another shallow bowl.
3. Dip the fish strips into the mayonnaise until well coated on all sides; now, roll them onto the seasoned breadcrumbs, pressing to adhere.
4. Sprinkle fish fingers with salt and pepper to taste; brush them with cooking oil.
5. Now, toss the cauliflower florets with salt, pepper, and celery seeds (if used). Add the fish fingers to the zone 1 drawer and the cauliflower florets to the zone 2 drawer.
6. Select zone 1 and pair it with "AIR FRY" at 200°C for 13 minutes. Select zone 2 and pair it with "AIR FRY" at 200°C for 20 minutes. Select "SYNC" followed by the "START/ STOP" button.
7. Shake the drawers halfway through the cooking time.

8. Once cooked, mash the cauliflower florets along with butter. Serve warm fish fingers with the cauliflower mash on the side. Garnish with scallions and enjoy!

Hot Sea Scallop and Pepper Salad

Serves 4

Prep time: 10 minutes / Cook time: 12 minutes

Ingredients

- 600g sea scallops
- 1 small knob of fresh root ginger, peeled and grated
- 1 tsp mustard seeds
- 1 large garlic clove, peeled
- 1 rosemary sprig, leaves picked
- 1 thyme sprig, leaves picked
- Sea salt and ground black pepper, to taste
- 1 medium lemon, freshly squeezed
- 2 tbsp extra-virgin olive oil
- 600g bell peppers, deveined and sliced
- 1 red chilli pepper, deveined and sliced
- 2 scallion stalks, chopped
- 1 head Romaine lettuce

Preparation instructions

1. Insert crisper plates in both drawers and spray them with cooking oil. Pat the sea scallops dry with paper towels.
2. Crush the ginger, mustard seeds, garlic, rosemary, and thyme using a pestle and mortar. Then, add salt, black pepper, 1 tablespoon of olive oil, and lemon juice; mix to combine well.
3. Rub the scallops with the spice/lemon mixture. Toss bell peppers with 1 tablespoon of olive oil, salt, black pepper, and red chilli

pepper.
4. Add the scallops to the zone 1 drawer and the bell peppers to the zone 2 drawer.
5. Select zone 1 and pair it with "AIR FRY" at 200°C for 8 minutes. Select zone 2 and pair it with "AIR FRY" at 200°C for 12 minutes. Select "SYNC" followed by the "START/ STOP" button.
6. Shake the drawers halfway through the cooking time. Toss your scallops with roasted bell peppers, scallions, and lettuce. Enjoy!

Calamari with Sweet Potatoes

Serves 4

Prep time: 10 minutes / Cook time: 20 minutes

Ingredients

- 400g squid, cleaned and cut into rings
- 1 tsp fresh ginger, peeled and minced
- 1 tbsp English mustard
- 2 tbsp soy sauce
- 100ml stout
- 80g all-purpose flour
- 1 medium egg
- 80g breadcrumbs
- 1 tsp garlic granules
- 1 tsp onion powder
- 1/2 tsp ground cumin
- 2 tsp olive oil
- 450g sweet potatoes, peeled and cut into 2.5cm chunks
- Sea salt and ground black pepper, to your liking

Preparation instructions

1. Insert crisper plates in both drawers and spray them with cooking oil.
2. Pat the squid rings dry with paper towels.

Add the squid, ginger, mustard, soy sauce, and stout to a ceramic or glass bowl. Cover and let it marinate in your fridge for about 1 hour. Discard the marinade.

3. Place the flour in a shallow dish. In a separate dish, whisk the egg until pale and frothy. Stir the breadcrumbs, garlic granules, onion powder, and ground cumin in a third shallow dish.

4. Dust the calamari rings in the flour. Then, dip them into the egg mixture; finally, coat them with the breadcrumb mixture; press to adhere on all sides. Drizzle the calamari rings with 1 teaspoon of olive oil.

5. Toss sweet potato chunks with salt, black pepper, and the remaining 1 teaspoon of olive oil.

6. Place calamari in the zone 1 drawer and sweet potatoes in the zone 2 drawer.

7. Select zone 1 and pair it with "AIR FRY" at 200°C for 10 minutes. Select zone 2 and pair it with "ROAST" at 200°C for 20 minutes. Select "SYNC" followed by the "START/ STOP" button.

8. Shake the drawers halfway through the cooking time. Serve calamari with roasted sweet potatoes. Enjoy!

Spicy Peppery Fish Patties

Serves 4

Prep time: 10 minutes / Cook time: 20 minutes

Ingredients

- 800g white fish fillets, boneless and flaked
- 1 medium onion, peeled and chopped
- 2 garlic cloves, pressed
- 1 bell pepper, seeded and chopped
- 1 small chilli pepper, chopped

- 2 slices of stale bread, crustless
- 2 tbsp milk
- 2 medium eggs, beaten
- 2 tbsp fresh parsley leaves, finely chopped
- Sea salt and ground black pepper, to taste
- 1 tsp paprika
- 100g plain flour
- 150g dried breadcrumbs

Preparation instructions

1. Insert crisper plates in both drawers. Line the crisper plates with baking parchment.

2. In a mixing bowl, thoroughly combine the flaked fish fillets, onion, garlic, bell pepper, chilli pepper, bread, milk, eggs, parsley, salt, black pepper, and paprika.

3. Then, add the flour and mix to combine well. Roll the fish mixture into small patties.

4. Place dried breadcrumbs in a shallow dish; then, roll the fish patties over the breadcrumbs; arrange fish patties on the prepared crisper plates.

5. Select zone 1 and pair it with "AIR FRY" at 200°C for 20 minutes. Select "MATCH" to duplicate settings across both zones. Press the "START/STOP" button.

6. When zone 1 time reaches 10 minutes, turn the fish patties over to ensure even cooking. Reinsert the drawers to continue cooking.

7. Bon appétit!

Garlicky Tiger Prawns with Aubergine

Serves 4

Prep time: 10 minutes / Cook time: 16 minutes

Ingredients

- 12 tiger prawns, peeled, tails on
- 1 tbsp butter, melted
- Juice of 1 lemon
- 1 tbsp stone-ground mustard
- 2 garlic cloves, pressed
- 1 tsp dried parsley flakes
- Sea salt and ground black pepper, to taste
- 1 tbsp olive oil
- 500g aubergine, cut in 2.5cm pieces

Preparation instructions

1. Insert crisper plates in both drawers. Spray the crisper plates with nonstick cooking oil.
2. Toss tiger prawns with butter, lemon juice, mustard, garlic, parsley, salt, and black pepper.
3. Toss aubergine pieces with salt and black pepper. Drizzle them with olive oil.
4. Place the prawns in the zone 1 drawer and the aubergine pieces in the zone 2 drawer.
5. Select zone 1 and pair it with "AIR FRY" at 200°C for 9 to 10 minutes. Select zone 2 and pair it with "AIR FRY" at 190°C for 15 to 16 minutes. Select "SYNC" followed by the "START/STOP" button.
6. When zone 1 time reaches 5 minutes, turn the prawns over using silicone-tipped tongs.
7. When zone 2 time reaches 8 minutes, shake the drawer and reinsert it to continue cooking.
8. Bon appétit!

Fish Fingers In Air Fryer

Serves 4

Prep time: 10 minutes / Cook time: 10 minutes

Ingredients

- 500g white fish fillets, cut into strips
- 80g all-purpose flour
- 2 eggs, beaten
- 100g breadcrumbs
- 1 tsp paprika
- 1/2 tsp garlic powder
- 1/2 tsp onion powder
- Salt and pepper, to taste
- Cooking spray

Preparation instructions

1. Preheat the Ninja Air Fryer to 200°C.
2. Set up a breading station with three shallow dishes. Place the flour in the first dish, the beaten eggs in the second dish, and the breadcrumbs, paprika, garlic powder, onion powder, salt, and pepper in the third dish. Mix the breadcrumb mixture until well combined.
3. Dip each fish strip in the flour, then the egg, and finally the breadcrumb mixture, making sure to coat the fish well at each step.
4. Spray the air fryer basket with cooking spray.
5. Place the breaded fish strips in the air fryer basket, making sure they are not touching.
6. Spray the tops of the fish strips with cooking spray.
7. Cook for 5 minutes, then flip the fish strips and cook for another 5 minutes, or until the fish is cooked through and the coating is golden brown and crispy.
8. Serve hot with your favourite dipping sauce.

Classic Fish Burgers

Serves 4

Prep time: 10 minutes / Cook time: 15 minutes

Ingredients

- 4 (160-170g each) sea bass fillets, skinless and boneless
- 1/2 tsp chilli flakes
- 1/2 tsp garlic granules
- Sea salt and ground black pepper, to taste
- 80g plain flour
- 1 large egg, beaten
- 100g fresh breadcrumbs
- 2 tsp olive oil
- 4 soft rolls
- 1 medium tomato, sliced
- A few lettuce leaves

Preparation instructions

1. Pat fish fillets dry using paper towels; then, coat the fish fillets in spices with your hands.
2. Now, create the breading station: Add the flour to a shallow bowl. Whisk the egg until it is well beaten. In a third shallow bowl, place the breadcrumbs.
3. Dust fish fillets with the flour. Dip fish fillets in the egg, and then, roll them over the breadcrumbs. Arrange the prepared fish fillets on the crisper plates in zone 1 and zone 2 drawers; brush them with olive oil.
4. Select zone 1 and pair it with "AIR FRY" at 200°C for 15 minutes. Select "MATCH" to duplicate settings across both zones. Press the "START/STOP" button.
5. When zone 1 time reaches 8 minutes, turn the fish fillets over to ensure even cooking. Reinsert the drawers to continue cooking.
6. Top warmed rolls with fish fillets, tomato, and fresh lettuce leaves. Bon appétit!

Air Fryer Fishcakes

Serves 4

Prep time: 10 minutes / Cook time: 35 minutes

Ingredients

- Cook The Fish
- 1 Pink Salmon Fillet
- 1 Cod Fillet
- 1 Pollock Fillet
- 2 Tsp Dill
- Salt & Pepper
- Cook The Potatoes
- 300 g Baby Potatoes
- 2 Tsp Extra Virgin Olive Oil
- Salt & Pepper
- 2 Tsp Butter
- Make The Production Line
- 2 Eggs beaten
- 480 ml Breadcrumbs
- 480 ml Plain Flour/All Purpose
- 2 Tbsp Lemon Juice
- 1 Tbsp Parsley
- 2 Tsp Dill Tops
- 2 Tsp Parsley
- 2 Tsp Basil
- Salt & Pepper
- Make The Fishcakes
- 1 Red Onion peeled and diced
- 2 Tsp Coriander
- 2 Tsp Parsley
- 2 Tsp Thyme
- 1 Tbsp Fresh Parsley shredded
- Salt & Pepper
- 1 Tbsp Butter

Preparation instructions

1. To remove any extra liquid, put the mixed fish fillets in a bowl and let them sit for an hour. You may first defrost them in the bowl

if they are frozen.

2. Then remove the fish (minus the excess water) and place on a chopping board. Season well with salt, pepper, and dill.

3. Load the fish into the air fryer and cook for 8 minutes at 180°C then place in bowl and use a fork to flake the fish.

4. In another bowl add baby potatoes, extra virgin olive oil and salt and pepper. Mix with your hands for an even coat. Air fry for 17 minutes at 180°C and then mash with a little butter. Add the mash to the cooked fish, along with a sliced red onion, and then add the fishcake seasoning list.

5. Use a fork or a masher to mash well and then add a little butter if you think it needs it. Then once cool enough to touch make into fish patties.

6. Though whilst you are waiting for them to cool set up your production line. Beaten egg in one bowl with lemon juice, flour and the 1tbsp of parsley in another bowl and the breadcrumbs and the rest of the seasoning in a third. Make sure all bowls are well mixed and that they are in the order of flour, egg, breadcrumbs.

7. Once you have made your patties load into the flour, into the egg and the breadcrumbs getting a good coating from each. Load into the Ninja Foodi air fryer basket and air fry for 10 minutes at 180°Cor until fully heated through and you have a crispy breadcrumb texture.

Vol Au Vent Cases

Serves 6

Prep time: 10 minutes / Cook time: 8 minutes

Ingredients

- 6 puff pastry vol-au-vent cases
- 200g prawns, peeled and deveined
- 50g mushrooms, finely chopped
- 1 small onion, finely chopped
- 1 garlic clove, minced
- 1 tbsp olive oil
- 1 tbsp flour
- 150ml milk
- 50g cheddar cheese, grated
- Salt and pepper, to taste
- Fresh parsley, chopped, for garnish

Preparation instructions

1. Preheat the Ninja Air Fryer to 180°C.

2. In a frying pan, heat the olive oil over medium heat. Add the onion and garlic and sauté for 2-3 minutes until softened.

3. Add the mushrooms and sauté for another 2-3 minutes.

4. Add the prawns to the pan and cook for 3-4 minutes until they turn pink.

5. Sprinkle the flour over the mixture and stir to coat evenly.

6. Gradually add the milk to the pan, stirring constantly until the mixture thickens.

7. Add the grated cheese and stir until melted and combined.

8. Season with salt and pepper to taste.

9. Spoon the mixture into the vol-au-vent cases.

10. Place the vol-au-vent cases in the air fryer basket and cook for 8 minutes or until the pastry is golden brown and crispy.

11. Garnish with chopped parsley and serve immediately.

Cajun Prawns

Serves 4

Prep time: 10 minutes / Cook time: 6 minutes

Ingredients

- 500g large raw prawns, peeled and deveined
- 2 tbsp olive oil
- 1 tsp Cajun seasoning
- 1/2 tsp garlic powder
- 1/2 tsp smoked paprika
- 1/4 tsp cayenne pepper
- Salt and pepper, to taste
- Fresh parsley, chopped, for garnish
- Lemon wedges, for serving

Preparation instructions

1. Preheat the Ninja Air Fryer to 200°C.
2. In a mixing bowl, combine the prawns, olive oil, Cajun seasoning, garlic powder, smoked paprika, cayenne pepper, salt, and pepper. Toss until the prawns are evenly coated.
3. Place the prawns in the air fryer basket and spread them out in a single layer.
4. Air fry the prawns for 6 minutes, shaking the basket halfway through cooking.
5. Remove the prawns from the air fryer and transfer them to a serving dish.
6. Garnish with chopped parsley and serve with lemon wedges on the side.

Note: Adjust the amount of Cajun seasoning and cayenne pepper according to your preference for spiciness. You can also serve the prawns with a dipping sauce or as a topping for salads or pasta dishes.

One-Pan Seafood Pilau

Serves 4

Prep time: 10 minutes / Cook time: 15 minutes

Ingredients

- 300g white fish, skinless, boneless and cut into strips
- 300g shrimp, cleaned and deveined
- 1 tbsp olive oil
- 2 bell peppers, deveined and chopped
- 200ml vegetable broth
- 1 (400g) can tomatoes, chopped
- 1 onion, chopped
- 2 garlic cloves, crushed or finely chopped
- 2 ancho chiles, chopped
- 2 tbsp olive oil
- 400g cooked rice
- 100g frozen sweet corn kernels, thawed

Preparation instructions

1. Mix the Ingredients until everything is well combined. Divide the mixture between two baking tins. Add baking tins to the drawers.
2. Select zone 1 and pair it with "ROAST" at 190°C for 15 minutes. Select "MATCH" to duplicate settings across both zones. Press the "START/STOP" button.
3. At the halfway point, stir your pilau with a wooden spoon and reinsert the drawers to resume cooking.
4. Allow your pilau to sit for about 10 minutes before serving. Devour!

Air Fryer White Fish

Serves 2-3

Prep time: 5 minutes / Cook time: 10-15 minutes

Ingredients

- 2-3 white fish fillets (such as cod or tilapia)
- 60g all-purpose flour
- 1/2 tsp garlic powder
- 1/2 tsp paprika
- Salt and pepper, to taste
- 1 large egg, beaten
- 50g panko bread crumbs
- Cooking spray

Preparation instructions

1. Preheat the Ninja Air Fryer to 200°C.
2. In a shallow bowl, mix the flour, garlic powder, paprika, salt, and pepper.
3. In another bowl, beat the egg.
4. In a third bowl, place the panko bread crumbs.
5. Dip each fish fillet into the flour mixture, shaking off any excess.
6. Then, dip the fish fillet into the beaten egg, coating both sides.
7. Finally, dip the fish fillet into the panko bread crumbs, pressing the crumbs onto the fish to coat well.
8. Place the breaded fish fillets in the air fryer basket.
9. Spray the tops of the fish with cooking spray.
10. Air fry the fish for 10-15 minutes, or until the fish is cooked through and the coating is crispy and golden brown.
11. Remove the fish from the air fryer basket and serve immediately.

Note: You can use any type of white fish fillets for this recipe.

Beer-Battered Prawn Tacos

Serves 4

Prep time: 10 minutes / Cook time: 16 minutes

Ingredients

- 400g prawns, cleaned and deveined
- 200g plain flour
- 1 (330ml) bottle of full-bodied beer
- Sea salt and ground black pepper, to taste
- 120g breadcrumbs
- 2 bell peppers, deveined and sliced
- 1 onion, peeled and cut into wedges
- 4 tbsp mayonnaise
- 4 tbsp salsa verde
- 8 small tortillas

Preparation instructions

1. Insert crisper plates in both drawers. Line crisper plates with baking paper.
2. Then, make the batter by tipping the flour, beer, salt and pepper into a bowl; now, slowly pour in the beer, whisking constantly until well combined. Add the breadcrumbs to another bowl.
3. Dredge your prawns in the batter and then roll them onto the breadcrumbs; press to adhere and arrange the prepared prawns on the crisper plates.
4. Place the prawns in the zone 1 drawer and the bell peppers along with onions in the zone 2 drawer.
5. Select zone 1 and pair it with "AIR FRY" at 200°C for 13 minutes. Select zone 2 and pair it with "ROAST" at 180°C for 16 minutes. Select "SYNC" followed by the "START/STOP" button.
6. Stir the Ingredients halfway through the cooking time.
7. Lastly, assemble your tacos with beer-battered prawns, roasted peppers, onions, mayo, and salsa verde. Enjoy!

Taco Cups

Serves 8

Prep time: 10 minutes / Cook time: 16 minutes

Ingredients

- 600g beef mince
- 1/2 tsp cumin powder
- 1 garlic clove, minced
- 4 rashers bacon, cut into halves lengthwise
- 2 medium eggs
- 100g cheddar cheese, grated
- 1 tsp dried basil
- 1 tsp dried oregano
- 1/2 tsp red pepper flakes, crushed
- Sea salt and ground black pepper, to taste

Preparation instructions

1. Start by preheating your Ninja Foodi to 180°C. Add beef mince, cumin powder, and garlic to a roasting tin.
2. Cook taco meat in the preheated Ninja Foodi for about 2 minutes; stir and break down the lumps with a wooden spatula and continue cooking for 2 minutes more, until no longer pink.
3. Line muffin cases with bacon rashers. Now, whisk the eggs for a few seconds and add the other Ingredients, including cooked beef mince.
4. Divide the taco mixture between prepared muffin cases. Add muffin cases to both drawers, without a crisper plate inserted.
5. Select zone 1 and pair it with "AIR FRY" at 190°C for 12 minutes. Select "MATCH" to duplicate settings across both zones. Press the "START/STOP" button.

6. Remove muffin cases from drawers and let them cool on a wire rack for approximately 10 minutes before unmolding and serving.
7. Bon appétit!

98 Lamb Chops with Root Vegetables

Serves 4

Prep time: 5 minutes / Cook time: 16 minutes

Ingredients

- 4 chops (120- 130g each) lamb chops
- 1 tsp garlic powder
- 1 tsp mustard seeds
- Sea salt and ground black pepper, to taste
- 1 tsp paprika
- 2 medium carrots, trimmed and cut into 1.5cm pieces
- 2 medium parsnips, trimmed and cut into 1.5cm pieces
- 1 tbsp olive oil

Preparation instructions

1. Insert a crisper plate into the zone 1 drawer. Spray the crisper plate with nonstick cooking oil.
2. Toss lamb chops and vegetables with spices and olive oil until they are well coated on all sides.
3. Place the lamb chops in the zone 1 drawer and the vegetables in the zone 2 drawer (with no crisper plate inserted).
4. Select zone 1 and pair it with "AIR FRY" at 200°C for 12 minutes. Select zone 2 and pair it with "ROAST" at 200°C for 16 minutes. Select "SYNC" followed by the "START/

STOP" button.

5. When zone 1 time reaches 6 minutes, turn the chops over and spray them with nonstick cooking oil on the other side; reinsert the drawer to continue cooking

6. When zone 2 time reaches 4 minutes, toss the drawer and reinsert it to continue cooking.

7. Bon appétit!

Air Fryer Brisket

Serves 4

Prep time: 5 minutes / Cook time: 45 minutes

Ingredients
- 1.2 kg Beef Brisket
- 2 Tsp Parsley
- 2 Tsp Rosemary
- 2 Tsp Thyme
- 1 Tbsp Extra Virgin Olive Oil
- 2 Tsp Basil
- Salt & Pepper

Preparation instructions

1. The simplest way to season your beef brisket and collect any particles of spice that have come off is to place it in a tray

2. Smoother after adding extra virgin olive oil, and smoother after adding spices. As the beef cooks, the dry spices will adhere to the oil and remain on the meat.

3. Roll the meat in the tray to collect any stray spice that may fall off.

4. After placing the Ingredients in the Ninja Foodi air fryer basket, cook for 30 minutes at 180°C.

5. Cook for a final 15 minutes at the same temperature after flipping. Now, it will be a medium.

Crackled Pork Belly with Green Beans

Serves 6

Prep time: 5 minutes + marinating time / Cook time: 50 minutes

Ingredients
- 1 large bay leaf
- 1 garlic clove, peeled
- 1 tbsp coriander seeds, crushed
- 1/2 tsp red pepper flakes
- Sea salt and ground black pepper, to taste
- 500g pork belly, boneless
- 500g green beans

Preparation instructions

1. Insert a crisper plate into the zone 1 drawer. Spray the crisper plate with nonstick cooking oil.

2. Crush bay leaf, garlic, coriander seeds, and red pepper flakes using a pestle and mortar; add salt, and black pepper, and mix to combine.

3. Rub the pork skin with the spice mixture using your hands until well coated on all sides; place the pork belly, covered, in your fridge and let it rest for at least 6 hours or overnight.

4. Select zone 1 and pair it with "AIR FRY" at 160°C for 50 minutes. Select zone 2 and pair it with "ROAST" at 200°C for 8 minutes. Select "SYNC" followed by the "START/ STOP" button.

5. When zone 1 time reaches 25 minutes, turn the pork belly over and then, reinsert the drawer to continue cooking

6. When zone 2 time reaches 4 minutes, toss the drawer and reinsert it to continue cooking.

7. Bon appétit!

Lamb with Broccoli Mash

Serves 4

Prep time: 10 minutes / Cook time: 20 minutes

Ingredients

- 3 steaks (300g each) of lamb steaks
- 1 tbsp Montreal seasoning mix
- Sea salt and ground black pepper, to taste
- 500g broccoli florets
- 1 tbsp butter, room temperature
- 2 tbsp fresh Italian parsley
- 1 tsp dried dill weed

Preparation instructions

1. Insert a crisper plate into zone 1. Spray the crisper plate with nonstick cooking oil.
2. Toss lamb steaks with the seasoning mix, olive oil, salt, and black pepper. Toss broccoli florets with salt and black pepper.
3. Place the lamb steaks in the zone 1 drawer and spray them with cooking oil; place the broccoli florets in the zone 2 drawer and spray them with cooking oil.
4. Select zone 1 and pair it with "AIR FRY" at 200°C for 15 minutes. Select zone 2 and pair it with "ROAST" at 200°C for 20 minutes. Select "SYNC" followed by the "START/STOP" button.
5. When zone 1 time reaches 8 minutes, turn the steaks over and spray them with nonstick cooking oil on the other side; reinsert the drawer to continue cooking.
6. When zone 2 time reaches 10 minutes, toss the broccoli florets to ensure even cooking and reinsert the drawer to continue cooking.
7. Add broccoli, butter, and dill to a bowl of your food processor; blitz using your blender or food processor to make a thick purée. Garnish broccoli mash with fresh parsley

leaves.
8. Add lamb steaks to a serving platter and serve them with the broccoli mash on the side. Bon appétit!

Pork Tenderloin with Roasted Pepper Salad

Serves 2

Prep time: 10 minutes / Cook time: 20 minutes

Ingredients

- 3 (200g each) pork tenderloin steaks
- 1 tbsp smoked paprika
- 1/2 tsp dried sage, crushed
- Sea salt and ground black pepper, to taste
- 4 bell peppers
- 1 tbsp extra-virgin olive oil
- 2 garlic cloves, peeled and minced
- 2 tbsp fresh parsley, chopped
- 2 tsp white vinegar

Preparation instructions

1. Insert a crisper plate into zone 1. Spray the crisper plate with nonstick cooking oil.
2. Spray the pork tenderloin with nonstick cooking oil. Toss pork tenderloin with smoked paprika, sage, salt, and black pepper.
3. Place the pork tenderloin steaks in the zone 1 drawer. Place the bell peppers in the zone 2 drawer (with no crisper plate inserted).
4. Select zone 1 and pair it with "AIR FRY" at 180°C for 18 minutes. Select zone 2 and pair it with "ROAST" at 200°C for 20 minutes. Select "SYNC" followed by the "START/STOP" button.
5. Remove the roasted peppers from the drawer and place them in a covered bowl for about 1 hour; now, remove the skin and stems from

your peppers and cut them into slices. Toss the peppers with olive oil, garlic, parsley, and vinegar.

6. Serve pork tenderloin with bell pepper salad and enjoy!

Air Fryer Pork Roast

Serves 4

Prep time:10 minutes / Cook time: 1h 20 minutes

Ingredients
- 1.2 kg Pork Shoulder
- 1 kg Air Fryer Sweet Potato Cubes
- 1 Tbsp Olive Oil
- 1 Tbsp Parsley
- 1 tsp Garlic Powder
- Salt & Pepper

Preparation instructions

1. Use square slits of a similar size to score the pork roast. Apply extra virgin olive oil as a mist. Add salt, pepper, and any additional Ingredients to the pork before cooking.
2. Make sure the rod has passed through both ends of the pork shoulder before inserting it. Each side's clamps should be secured.
3. Make sure it is secure before placing it in the Ninja Foodi air fryer oven. Time and temperature should be set at 1 hour and 180 C/360 F, accordingly. Remove from the air fryer and rest when it beeps.
4. Remove the clamps and rod when it has rested for about 5 minutes, then let it sit without cutting for another 5 minutes.

Sizzling BBQ Ribs

Serves 5

Prep time: 5 minutes / Cook time: 45 minutes

Ingredients
- 1 kg pork back ribs, bone-in and trimmed
- BBQ Sauce:
- 200ml tomato sauce
- 2 tbsp olive oil
- 50ml Appleton rum
- 1 garlic clove, crushed
- 1 Scotch bonnet chilli, seeded and chopped
- 50g honey
- Sea salt and ground black pepper, to taste

Preparation instructions

1. Pat the back ribs dry with tea towels. In a mixing bowl, thoroughly combine all the Ingredients for the BBQ sauce.
2. Toss the ribs with the BBQ sauce and divide them between lightly greased drawers of your Ninja Foodi.
3. Select zone 1 and pair it with "AIR FRY" at 190°C for 45 minutes. Select "MATCH" to duplicate settings across both zones. Press the "START/STOP" button.
4. At the halfway point, flip the back ribs with silicone-tipped tongs and brush them with the reserved BBQ sauce. Reinsert drawers to resume cooking.
5. Bon appétit!

Festive Meatloaf

Serves 6

Prep time: 10 minutes / Cook time: 22 minutes

Ingredients

- 400g pork mince
- 400g beef mince
- 1 thick stale bread slice
- 1 large egg, beaten
- 1 medium leek, chopped
- 2 garlic cloves, minced
- 1 tbsp dried parsley flakes
- 1 tsp red pepper flakes, crushed
- 100g cornflakes, crushed
- 1 tbsp butter
- 200ml tomato paste
- 1 tbsp maple syrup
- 1 tbsp Dijon mustard

Preparation instructions

1. Brush two loaf tins with nonstick cooking oil.
2. In a mixing bowl, thoroughly combine the pork mince, beef mince, bread slice, egg, leek, garlic, parsley, red pepper flakes, cornflakes, and butter.
3. Scrape the mixture into the prepared loaf tins. Brush the meatloaves with cooking oil. Add a loaf tin to each drawer.
4. Mix the tomato paste, maple syrup, and mustard; reserve.
5. Select zone 1 and pair it with "AIR FRY" at 180°C for 22 minutes. Select "MATCH" to duplicate settings across both zones. Press the "START/STOP" button.
6. When zone 1 time reaches 11 minutes, spread the tomato mixture over the top of your meatloaves and bake for a further 11 minutes, until the centre of your meatloaf reaches 74°C. Reinsert the drawer to continue cooking.
7. Let your meatloaves rest for 10 minutes on a wire rack before slicing and serving. Bon appétit!

Beef Hot Pot

Serves 5

Prep time: 10 minutes / Cook time: 25 minutes

Ingredients

- 600g beef stew meat, cut into bite-sized pieces
- 1 tbsp olive oil
- 100ml red wine
- 1 tbsp Dijon mustard
- 1 tbsp fresh ginger, peeled and grated
- 2 tbsp plain flour
- 1 medium onion, peeled and sliced
- 1 large carrot, trimmed and sliced
- 2 bell peppers, seeded and sliced
- 2 garlic cloves, finely sliced

Preparation instructions

1. Place the beef meat, olive oil, wine, mustard, and ginger in a ceramic dish; cover the dish and allow the meat to marinate for approximately 2 hours in your fridge. Discard the marinade.
2. Toss the beef pieces with plain flour and add them to the lightly-greased baking tin.
3. Add the other Ingredients to the baking tin. Gently stir to combine and cover the baking tin with foil (with the shiny side down). Place the baking tins in both drawers.
4. Select zone 1 and pair it with "AIR FRY" at 180°C for 25 minutes. Select "MATCH" to duplicate settings across both zones. Press the "START/STOP" button.
5. Enjoy!

Greek Steak Salad

Serves 6

Prep time: 10 minutes / Cook time: 25 minutes

Ingredients

- 6 (180-200g each) rib eye steak
- 1 tsp dried oregano
- 1 tsp dried thyme
- 1 tsp dried sage
- Sea salt and ground black pepper, to taste
- 1 tbsp extra-virgin olive oil
- 1 small head of lettuce
- 100g cherry tomatoes, halved
- 1 small cucumber, peeled and diced
- 1 small avocado, peeled, pitted, and sliced
- 100g Kalamata olives, pitted and sliced
- 50g feta cheese, crumbled

Preparation instructions

1. Insert the crisper plates in both drawers and spray them with cooking oil.
2. Toss the steaks with oregano, thyme, sage, salt, and black pepper in a resealable bag; give them a good shake until everything is well covered.
3. Place the steaks in both drawers.
4. Select zone 1 and pair it with "AIR FRY" at 200°C for 25 minutes. Select "MATCH" to duplicate settings across both zones. Press the "START/STOP" button.
5. When zone 1 time reaches 15 minutes, turn the steaks over and reinsert the drawer to continue cooking.
6. Cut your steak into strips and add them to a salad bowl; add the remaining Ingredients for the salad, and toss to combine. Serve your salad at room temperature and enjoy!

108 Old-Fashioned Pilaf

Serves 4

Prep time: 10 minutes / Cook time: 30 minutes

Ingredients

- 400g beef mince
- 200g pork sausage, chopped
- 1 onion, chopped
- 300ml vegetable broth
- 1 (400g) can tomatoes, chopped
- 2 garlic cloves, crushed or finely chopped
- 2 tbsp olive oil
- 400g cooked rice
- 100g frozen green peas, thawed

Preparation instructions

1. In a mixing bowl, thoroughly combine the beef mince, sausage, onion, and 100 ml of vegetable broth. Divide the mixture between two baking tins. Add baking tins to the drawers.
2. Select zone 1 and pair it with "AIR FRY" at 190°C for 15 minutes. Select "MATCH" to duplicate settings across both zones. Press the "START/STOP" button.
3. At the halfway point, stir the meat with a wooden spoon and reinsert the drawers to resume cooking.
4. Once cooked, add the other Ingredients to the baking tins. Gently stir to combine.
5. Select zone 1 and pair it with "ROAST" at 190°C for 15 minutes. Select "MATCH" to duplicate settings across both zones. Press the "START/STOP" button.
6. Bon appétit!

Pork Medallions with Green Bean Salad

Serves 4

Prep time: 10 minutes / Cook time: 18 minutes

Ingredients

- 4 (120g each) pork medallions
- 1 tsp dried parsley flakes
- Sea salt and ground black pepper, to taste
- 500g green beans
- 2 tbsp olive oil
- 100ml mayonnaise
- 1 tbsp Dijon mustard
- 1 pickle, chopped

Preparation instructions

1. Toss pork medallions with 1 tablespoon of olive oil and spices until they are well coated on both sides. Arrange pork medallions in a lightly-greased drawer (with a crisper plate).
2. Toss green beans with olive oil and place them in zone 2 drawer (without a crisper plate).
3. Select zone 1 and pair it with "AIR FRY" at 190°C for 18 minutes. Select zone 2 and pair it with "ROAST" at 200°C for 10 minutes. Select "SYNC" followed by the "START/ STOP" button.
4. When zone 1 time reaches 9 minutes, turn the pork medallions over and reinsert the drawer to continue cooking.
5. When zone 2 time reaches 5 minutes, toss the drawer and reinsert the drawer to continue cooking.
6. Mix green beans with mayonnaise, mustard, and pickle. Serve pork medallions with creamed green bean salad.
7. Bon appétit!

Air Fryer Rump Steak

Serves 2

Prep time: 10 minutes / Cook time: 10-12 minutes

Ingredients

- 2 rump steaks, about 200-250g each
- 1 tsp olive oil
- 1 tsp garlic powder
- 1 tsp onion powder
- 1 tsp dried thyme
- Salt and black pepper, to taste

Preparation instructions

1. Preheat the Ninja Air Fryer to 200°C.
2. Rub the steaks with olive oil and seasonings, coating them evenly on all sides.
3. Place the steaks in the air fryer basket.
4. Air fry the steaks for 5-6 minutes on one side, then flip them over.
5. Continue to air fry the steaks for another 5-6 minutes on the other side.
6. Check the internal temperature of the steaks with a meat thermometer. For medium-rare steaks, the internal temperature should be around 60°C; for medium, it should be around 65-70°C.
7. Remove the steaks from the air fryer basket and let them rest for 5-10 minutes before slicing and serving.

Paprika Gammon Steaks

Serves 6

Prep time: 10 minutes / Cook time: 20 minutes

Ingredients

- 6 (225g each) gammon steaks
- 3 tsp smoked paprika
- 1 tsp garlic granules

- Sea salt and ground black pepper, to taste
- 1 tbsp olive oil

Preparation instructions

1. Insert a crisper plate into the zone 1 and zone 2 drawers. Spray the crisper plates with nonstick cooking oil.
2. Toss gammon steaks with smoked paprika, garlic granules, salt, black pepper, and olive oil.
3. Place gammon steaks in zone 1 and zone 2 drawers.
4. Select zone 1 and pair it with "AIR FRY" at 180°C for 20 minutes. Select "MATCH" to duplicate settings across both zones. Press the "START/STOP" button.
5. At the halfway point, turn the gammon steaks over and reinsert the drawers to resume cooking.
6. Bon appétit!

Grandma's Famous Roast Beef

Serves 5

Prep time: 10 minutes / Cook time: 40 minutes

Ingredients

- 1 kg beef roast (topside of beef), cut into two pieces
- 1 tbsp olive oil
- 1 tbsp sage
- 1 tbsp rosemary
- Sea salt and ground black pepper, to taste
- 1 tsp cayenne pepper
- 4 medium carrots, cut into rounds
- 2 sticks celery, peeled and diced
- 1 bulb of garlic, break it into cloves, unpeeled

Preparation instructions

1. Insert crisper plates in both drawers. Rub beef pieces with olive oil, herbs, salt, black pepper, and cayenne pepper.
2. Now, place the beef in the zone 1 drawer and vegetables in the zone 2 drawer; then, insert drawers in the unit.
3. Select zone 1 and pair it with "AIR FRY" at 185°C for 40 minutes. Select zone 2 and pair it with "ROAST" at 200°C for 16 minutes. Select "SYNC" followed by the "START/ STOP" button.
4. When zone 1 time reaches 20 minutes, turn the beef over and reinsert the drawer to continue cooking.
5. When zone 2 time reaches 8 minutes, toss the drawer and reinsert it to continue cooking.
6. Cover the warm roast beef with tin foil and tea towels; allow the roast beef to rest for about 10 minutes before carving and serving. Serve the roast beef with vegs on the side and enjoy!

Marinated London Broil

Serves 5

Prep time: 10 minutes + marinating time / Cook time: 35 minutes

Ingredients

- 1kg London broil, cut into 2 pieces
- 2 tsp olive oil
- 1 tbsp English mustard
- 150ml dry red wine
- 2 garlic cloves, pressed
- 1 thyme sprig
- 1 bay leaf
- 1 rosemary sprig
- 1 tsp red pepper flakes
- Sea salt and ground black pepper, to taste

Preparation instructions

1. In a ceramic dish, place London broil, olive oil, mustard, wine, garlic, thyme, leaf, rosemary, red pepper, salt, and black pepper; let it marinate for 2 hours in your refrigerator.
2. Add London broil to both drawers (with crisper plates inserted).
3. Select zone 1 and pair it with "AIR FRY" at 185°C for 35 minutes. Select "MATCH" to duplicate settings across both zones. Press the "START/STOP" button.
4. At the halfway point, turn the meat over and reinsert the drawers to resume cooking.
5. Bon appétit!

Traditional Greek Gyro

Serves 4

Prep time: 10 minutes / Cook time: 50 minutes

Ingredients

- 500g Boston butt, boneless and excessive fat removed, cut into strips
- 1 tsp garlic powder
- 1 tsp onion powder
- 1/2 tsp cumin powder
- 1 tsp cayenne pepper
- Sea salt and ground black pepper, to taste
- 400g potatoes, peeled and cut into thin chips
- 2 tbsp olive oil
- 4 tbsp tzatziki
- 1 medium tomato, sliced
- 1 medium red onion, sliced
- 4 large pita bread

Preparation instructions

1. Place Boston butt with the spices and 1 tbsp of olive oil in a resealable bag; give it a good shake until the meat pieces are well coated with spices.

2. Toss potato chips with the remaining 1 tablespoon of olive oil, salt, and black pepper.
3. Now, place the beef in the zone 1 drawer and the potatoes in the zone 2 drawer; then, insert drawers in the unit.
4. Select zone 1 and pair it with "AIR FRY" at 180°C for 50 minutes. Select zone 2 and pair it with "AIR FRY" at 200°C for 22 minutes. Select "SYNC" followed by the "START/STOP" button.
5. When zone 1 time reaches 25 minutes, shake the drawer and reinsert it to continue cooking.
6. When zone 2 time reaches 11 minutes, shake the drawer and reinsert it to continue cooking.
7. Afterwards, serve pork on pita bread with tzatziki, tomatoes, and red onion. Enjoy!

Beef Wellington

Serves 2

Prep time: 40 minutes / Cook time: 40 minutes

Ingredients

- 2 tsp Dijon mustard
- 1 sheet frozen puff pastry, just thawed
- 1 egg, lightly whisked
- Steamed broccolini, to serve
- Onion relish, to serve
- 1 tbsp olive oil
- 2 x 3.5cm-thick (about 150g each) beef eye fillet steaks
- 200g button mushrooms, finely chopped
- 2 French shallots, peeled, finely chopped
- 2 garlic cloves, crushed
- 7 slices prosciutto

Preparation instructions

1. In a big frying pan, heat the oil over high heat. Cook the steaks for 3–4 minutes on each side, turning once, or until just lightly browned. Transfer to a platter and chill a little in the refrigerator.

2. heat to a medium level. Add shallot, garlic, and mushrooms to the pan. Cook for 15 minutes while stirring often, or until golden and liquid has evaporated. Place on a platter. Place in refrigerator for five minutes, or until just just cold.

3. On a piece of plastic wrap, arrange six slices of prosciutto, gently overlapping each other to form a rectangle. With a thin border, spread the mushie mixture over top. Place the steaks on top of the rectangle, lengthwise. Apply mustard on steaks. Overlap the steaks with the prosciutto. To fill up any gaps, place the remaining prosciutto slice lengthwise on top. Embrace ends. securely wrap with plastic wrap. Place in the refrigerator to cool for 20 minutes.

4. On a level surface, spread out the pastry. Unwrap the log, then place it on the crust. To enclose, fold pastry over and tuck ends under to seal. Place on a sheet of baking paper, seam-side down. After eggwashing the top, score the pastry diagonally with a knife.

5. Place in the basket of your Ninja Foodi air fryer. Cook until desired doneness is achieved, around 20 minutes at 180°C for medium rare. Serve with relish and broccolini.

Hot and Spicy Chuck Steak

Serves 4

Prep time: 10 minutes + marinating time / Cook time: 22 minutes

Ingredients

- 1kg top chuck steaks
- 1 tbsp English mustard
- 2 tbsp soy sauce
- 2 tbsp sherry vinegar
- Sea salt and ground black pepper, to taste
- 1 tsp hot paprika
- 1 tsp red pepper flakes, crushed
- 1 tsp dried basil
- 2 tsp olive oil

Preparation instructions

1. Toss top chuck with the remaining Ingredients in a resealable bag; shake to coat well and allow it to marinate for at least 2 hours.

2. Add chuck steaks to both drawers.

3. Select zone 1 and pair it with "AIR FRY" at 200°C for 22 minutes. Select "MATCH" to duplicate settings across both zones. Press the "START/STOP" button.

4. At the halfway point, turn the meat over and reinsert the drawers to resume cooking.

5. Bon appétit!

CHAPTER 7 SNACKS & APPETIZERS

Meatballs with Hot Dipping Sauce

Serves 5

Prep time: 10 minutes / Cook time: 20 minutes

Ingredients
- Meatballs:
- 500g turkey mince, 93% lean and 7% fat
- 300g pork mince
- 120g porridge oats
- 2 cloves garlic, minced
- 1 medium egg, beaten
- 1 tsp ground cumin
- 1 tsp coriander seeds
- Sea salt and ground black pepper, to taste
- 1 tbsp olive oil
- Dipping Sauce:
- 20ml honey
- 100ml hot sauce
- 2 tbsp butter

Preparation instructions
1. In a mixing bowl, thoroughly combine all the Ingredients for the meatballs. Shape the mixture into equal balls.
2. Select zone 1 and pair it with "AIR FRY" at 185°C for 20 minutes. Select "MATCH" to duplicate settings across both zones. Press the "START/STOP" button.
3. At the halfway point, turn the meatballs over and reinsert the drawers to resume cooking.
4. Preheat a saucepan over medium-high heat; melt the butter and then, add hot sauce and honey.
5. Serve warm meatballs with cocktail sticks and dipping sauce on the side.
6. Bon appétit!

The Best Wings Ever

Serves 4

Prep time: 5 minutes + marinating time / Cook time: 33 minutes

Ingredients
- 1 kg chicken wings, drumettes & flats
- 1 tbsp butter, melted
- 1/2 tsp ground cumin
- 1 tsp garlic powder
- 2 tbsp Worcestershire sauce
- 1 tsp hot paprika
- 2 tbsp golden syrup
- Sea salt and ground black pepper, to taste

Preparation instructions
1. Place all the Ingredients in a ceramic bowl. Give them a good stir, cover the bowl, and let the chicken wings marinate for approximately 1 hour in the fridge.
2. Drain and reserve the marinade.
3. Insert crisper plates in both drawers. Spray the crisper plates with nonstick cooking oil. Divide the chicken wings between drawers.
4. Select zone 1 and pair it with "AIR FRY" at 200°C for 33 minutes. Select "MATCH
5. At the halfway point, turn the wings over, and baste them with the reserved marinade.
6. Bon appétit!

Burnt Butter Cabbage

Serves 5

Prep time: 10 minutes / Cook time: 15 minutes

Ingredients
- 1kg pointed cabbage, cut into wedges

- 2 tbsp butter, melted
- Sea salt and ground black pepper, to taste
- 1 tsp garlic granules
- 1 tsp paprika
- 1/2 lemon, juiced and zested

Preparation instructions

1. Insert crisper plates in both drawers. Spray the crisper plates with nonstick cooking oil.
2. Gently toss cabbage wedges with the other Ingredients. Divide the cabbage wedges between drawers.
3. Select zone 1 and pair it with "AIR FRY" at 190°C for 15 minutes. Select "MATCH" followed by the "START/STOP" button.
4. At the halfway point, turn the cabbage over to ensure even cooking; reinsert the drawers to resume cooking.
5. Bon appétit!

Cheese Quiche

Serves 4

Prep time: 15 minutes / Cook time: 18 minutes

Ingredients

- 300 g Air Fryer Pie Crust
- 300 g Grated Cheddar Cheese
- 4 Cherry Tomatoes
- 75 ml Whole Milk
- 3 Large Eggs
- 1 Tbsp Oregano
- 2 Tsp Mixed Herbs
- Salt & Pepper

Preparation instructions

1. Make your pie crust first. Add mixed herbs to the crust to enhance the flavor. Roll out into ramekins or other like containers.
2. Salt and pepper are added while you combine the milk and eggs in a mixing dish.
3. When the ramekins are little more than 3/4 full, pour the milk and egg mixture over the cheese that has been shredded. The mixture should be topped with cherry tomatoes that have been sliced in half. Oregano and more cheese should be included as well.
4. The suggested air-frying duration is 8 minutes at 180°C/360°F, followed by another 10 minutes at 160°C

Creamy Beet Salad

Serves 5

Prep time: 10 minutes + chilling time / Cook time: 40 minutes

Ingredients

- 1kg red beets, peeled, whole
- 1 tbsp extra-virgin olive oil
- 1 tbsp white vinegar
- 1 tsp stone-ground mustard
- 1/2 tsp cumin, ground
- Sea salt and ground black pepper, to taste
- 1 small bulb of garlic
- 1/2 small bunch parsley, roughly chopped
- 1 medium avocado

Preparation instructions

1. Insert crisper plates in both drawers. Spray the crisper plates with nonstick cooking oil. Place the beets in both drawers of your Ninja Foodi.
2. Select zone 1 and pair it with "AIR FRY" at 200°C for 40 minutes. Select "MATCH" followed by the "START/STOP" button.
3. At the halfway point, turn the beets over to ensure even cooking; wrap the garlic bulb in foil and place it in the zone 1 drawer. Now, reinsert the drawers to resume cooking.

4. In the meantime, place the avocado halves on a cutting board; now, whack the pit with the sharp end of the knife to remove it easily. Use a spoon to scoop avocado flesh; chop your avocado and set it aside.

5. Now, pull or squeeze the roasted garlic cloves out of their skins; mash them with a fork.

6. Let the beets cool and remove the skin. Cut your beets into slices and toss them with the remaining Ingredients, including avocado and roasted garlic. Enjoy!

Pizza Rolls

Serves 4

Prep time: 5 minutes / Cook time: 10 minutes

Ingredients

- 500 gPizza Dough
- 4 Tbsp Pizza Sauce
- 150 g Hard Cheese
- 50 g Grated Gouda
- 8 Tsp Soft Cheese
- 2 Tsp Oregano
- 1 Tsp Basil
- Egg Wash optional

Preparation instructions

1. Roll out your pizza dough and using a pizza cutter, cut it into 8 equal pizza slices.

2. Layer it with pizza sauce, a teaspoon of soft cheese and stick your hard cheese to it. Add some grated cheese too.

3. Roll it from the biggest to the smallest part until you have 8 croissant shaped pizza rolls. Cover the tops with egg wash.

4. Place the pizza rolls into a baking tray and add the baking tray to the middle shelf of your air fryer oven. Cook at 180°C for 10 minutes. Serve warm.

Butter-Fried Asparagus

Serves 5

Prep time: 10 minutes / Cook time: 15 minutes

Ingredients

- 1kg asparagus spears, trimmed
- 2 tbsp butter, melted
- 2 garlic cloves, pressed
- 1 tsp dried dill weed
- 1 tsp paprika
- Sea salt and ground black pepper, to taste
- 1/2 lemon, juiced and zested

Preparation instructions

1. In a mixing dish, toss asparagus with the other Ingredients until well coated in butter and aromatics.

2. Add asparagus to both drawers of your Ninja Foodi (with a crisper plate inserted).

3. Select zone 1 and pair it with "AIR FRY" at 200°C for 15 minutes. Select "MATCH" followed by the "START/STOP" button.

4. At the halfway point, stir the Ingredients to ensure even cooking; reinsert the drawers to resume cooking.

5. Bon appétit!

Okra Chips with Lemon Mayonnaise

Serves 5

Prep time: 15 minutes / Cook time: 20 minutes

Ingredients

- 1kg okra, cut into halves lengthwise
- 1 tbsp extra-virgin olive oil
- 1 tsp garlic granules
- 1 tsp onion powder
- 1 tsp ground coriander

- 1 tsp turmeric powder
- Sea salt and ground black pepper, to taste
- 100g breadcrumbs
- Lemon Mayonaisse:
- 2 egg yolks
- 1 tsp Dijon mustard
- 1 tbsp balsamic vinegar
- 1 salted anchovy
- 200ml olive oil
- 1 lemon, freshly squeezed
- 1 tsp dried dill weed
- Sea salt and red pepper, to taste

Preparation instructions

1. Toss okra halves with olive oil, spices, and breadcrumbs until they are well coated on all sides.
2. Add okra to both drawers of your Ninja Foodi (with a crisper plate inserted).
3. Select zone 1 and pair it with "AIR FRY" at 180°C for 20 minutes. Select "MATCH" followed by the "START/STOP" button.
4. At the halfway point, shake the drawers to ensure even cooking; reinsert the drawers to resume cooking.
5. Meanwhile, make the lemon mayonnaise. Add egg yolks, mustard, vinegar, and anchovy to a bowl of your food processor; process until smooth paste forms.
6. Slowly and gradually, pour in the olive oil until the mixture becomes glossy and slightly thick. To finish, add lemon juice, dill, salt, and red pepper, and blitz for a few seconds more, until well combined.
7. Serve okra chips with lemon mayonnaise on the side and enjoy!

Griddled Aubergine Rounds

Serves 5

Prep time: 10 minutes / Cook time: 15 minutes

Ingredients

- 3 medium aubergines, cut into 1cm-thick slices
- 1 tbsp olive oil
- Sea salt and ground black pepper, to taste
- 1 tsp cayenne pepper
- 1 tsp dried dill weed
- 1/2 tsp sumac
- 200g Parmesan cheese, grated

Preparation instructions

1. Insert crisper plates in both drawers. Spray the crisper plates with nonstick cooking oil.
2. Toss aubergines with olive oil, salt, black pepper, cayenne pepper, dill, and sumac. Arrange the aubergine rounds in both drawers of your Ninja Foodi.
3. Select zone 1 and pair it with "AIR FRY" at 190°C for 15 minutes. Select "MATCH" followed by the "START/STOP" button.
4. At the halfway point, turn aubergine rounds over and top them with cheese; reinsert the drawers to resume cooking.
5. Bon appétit!

Courgette Fritters

Serves 5

Prep time: 10 minutes / Cook time: 20 minutes

Ingredients

- 400g courgette, grated
- 200g plain flour
- 2 medium eggs, beaten
- 1 small onion, chopped

- 1/2 lemon, zested
- 50g Parmesan cheese, grated
- 1/2 tsp dried dill
- Sea salt and ground black pepper, to taste
- 1 tsp paprika
- 1 tsp dried oregano
- 1 tbsp olive oil

Preparation instructions

1. Insert crisper plates in both drawers. Spray the crisper plates with nonstick cooking oil.
2. Toss the courgette with 1 teaspoon of coarse sea salt in a colander; let it sit for about 15 minutes; after that, squeeze out the excess moisture using tea towels.
3. Thoroughly combine grated courgette with the remaining Ingredients. Shape the mixture into small patties and arrange them in both drawers.
4. Select zone 1 and pair it with "AIR FRY" at 190°C for 20 minutes. Select "MATCH" followed by the "START/STOP" button.
5. At the halfway point, turn the courgette fritters over, and reinsert the drawers to resume cooking.
6. Bon appétit!

The Best Pigs-in-Blankets Ever

Serves 6

Prep time: 10 minutes / Cook time: 15 minutes

Ingredients

- 12 cocktail sausages, casing removed
- 6 rashers pancetta, cut into halves lengthwise
- 1 tsp hot paprika

Preparation instructions

1. Insert crisper plates in both drawers. Spray the crisper plates with nonstick cooking oil.

2. Wrap sausages in the pancetta slices and arrange them in both drawers if your Ninja Foodi.
3. Select zone 1 and pair it with "AIR FRY" at 180°C for 15 minutes. Select "MATCH" followed by the "START/STOP" button.
4. At the halfway point, turn the pigs-in-blankets over, and reinsert the drawers to resume cooking.
5. Sprinkle warm pigs-in-blankets with hot paprika and enjoy!

Mozzarella Sticks

Serves 6

Prep time: 10 minutes / Cook time: 8 minutes

Ingredients

- 400g block firm mozzarella cheese, cut into 1cm-thick finger-length strips
- 100g all-purpose flour
- 1 medium egg
- 150g breadcrumbs
- 1 tsp garlic granules
- 1 tsp dried parsley flakes
- Sea salt and cayenne pepper, to your liking
- 1 tbsp olive oil

Preparation instructions

1. Insert crisper plates in both drawers. Spray the crisper plates with nonstick cooking oil.
2. Next, set up your breading station. Place all-purpose flour in a shallow dish. In a separate dish, whisk the egg. Lastly, thoroughly combine the breadcrumbs with garlic granules, parsley flakes, salt, and cayenne pepper in a third dish.
3. Start by dredging mozzarella sticks in the flour; then, dip them into the egg. Press mozzarella sticks into the breadcrumb mixture.

4. Brush breaded mozzarella sticks with olive oil and arrange them in both drawers.

5. Select zone 1 and pair it with "AIR FRY" at 190°C for 8 minutes. Select "MATCH" followed by the "START/STOP" button.

6. At the halfway point, turn the mozzarella sticks over to ensure even cooking; reinsert the drawers to resume cooking.

7. Serve mozzarella sticks with a dipping sauce of your choice, and enjoy!

8. Bon appétit!

Stuffed Mushrooms

Serves 4

Prep time: 10 minutes / Cook time: 13 minutes

Ingredients

- 8 medium portobello mushrooms
- 50g butter, room temperature
- 180g feta cheese, pressed and crumbled
- 1 bell pepper, seeded and chopped
- 1 garlic clove, minced
- 2 scallion stalks, chopped
- Sea salt and ground black pepper, to taste
- 1 tbsp olive oil

Preparation instructions

1. Insert crisper plates in both drawers. Spray the crisper plates with nonstick cooking oil.

2. Pat the mushrooms dry with paper (or tea) towels and remove the stems; chop the stems and reserve.

3. Add the mushroom stems, butter, cheese, bell pepper, garlic, scallions, salt, and black pepper to a mixing bowl. Stir to combine and divide the filling between portobello mushrooms.

4. Place the stuffed mushrooms in both drawers and brush them with olive oil.

5. Select zone 1 and pair it with "AIR FRY" at 185°C for 13 minutes. Select "MATCH" followed by the "START/STOP" button.

6. Bon appétit!

Potato Latkes

Serves 4

Prep time: 10 minutes / Cook time: 15 minutes

Ingredients

- 4 large potatoes, scrubbed
- 1 onion, peeled and chopped
- 1 garlic clove, minced
- 2 medium eggs, beaten
- 4 tbsp plain flour
- 1 tbsp cilanotro (or parsley)
- 1 tbsp rosemary
- Sea salt and ground black pepper, to taste
- 1 tbsp olive oil

Preparation instructions

1. Insert crisper plates in both drawers. Spray the crisper plates with nonstick cooking oil.

2. Coarsely grate your potatoes with skin. Now, wring out the liquid with a clean tea towel. (Maris Piper potatoes work best).

3. Add the other Ingredients to the grated potatoes. Shape the mixture into latkes, flattening gently with a wide spatula (or fork).

4. Arrange potato lathes in both drawers of your Ninja Foodi.

5. Select zone 1 and pair it with "AIR FRY" at 180°C for 15 minutes. Select "MATCH" followed by the "START/STOP" button. Flip potato latkes halfway through the cooking time.

6. Bon appétit!

Stuffed Mushrooms

/Serves 16 bites

Prep time: 5 minutes / Cook time: 8 minutes

Ingredients

- 16 oz Mini/Baby Portobello Mushrooms
- 1 lb Mild Ground Pork Sausage Cooked and Drained
- 8 oz Package of Cream Cheese Softened
- 2 Tbsp Fresh Chopped Parsley
- 1 Garlic Clove Crushed
- 80g Grated Parmesan Cheese

Preparation instructions

1. Take off the stems and clean the mushrooms. In a food processor, add the stems.
2. The food processor should be filled with the cooked sausage, cream cheese, parsley, garlic clove, and cheese. Blend until the Ingredients are well chopped.
3. Apply olive oil cooking spray on the foil or air fryer basket.
4. Place each mushroom on the foil or basket after stuffing it. Apply a second application of cooking spray evenly.
5. 8 minutes of cooking at 390 degrees in the air fryer. Remove and serve with care.

Green Bean Chips with Homemade Mayo Dip

Serves 5

Prep time: 15 minutes / Cook time: 10 minutes

Ingredients

- 1 kg green beans, trimmed
- 1 tbsp olive oil, divided
- 1 tsp garlic granules
- 1 tsp onion powder
- 1 tsp dried oregano
- Sea salt and black pepper, to taste
- 200g Parmesan cheese, preferably freshly grated
- Mayo Dip:
- 2 egg yolks
- 1 tsp English mustard
- 1 tbsp white vinegar
- 200ml olive oil
- 1 lemon, freshly squeezed
- 1 tbsp Greek spice mix

Preparation instructions

1. Toss green beans with olive oil and spices. Add green beans to both drawers (with a crisper plate inserted).
2. Select zone 1 and pair it with "AIR FRY" at 200°C for 10 minutes. Select "MATCH" followed by the "START/STOP" button.
3. When zone 1 time reaches 5 minutes, shake the drawer and toss green beans with Parmesan cheese. Reinsert the drawer to continue cooking.
4. Meanwhile, make the mayo dip. Add egg yolks, mustard, and vinegar to a bowl of your food processor; process until smooth paste forms.
5. Slowly and gradually, pour in the olive oil until the mixture becomes glossy and slightly thick. To finish, add lemon juice and Greek spice mix; mix for a few seconds more, until well combined.
6. Serve green bean chips with your homemade mayo dip on the side and enjoy!

Aubergine Burgers

Serves 4

Prep time: 10 minutes / Cook time: 15 minutes

Ingredients
- 1 large aubergine, wide middle section cut into 8 rounds
- 1 tbsp olive oil
- 1 tsp stone-ground mustard
- 1/2 tsp ground cumin
- Sea salt and ground black pepper, to taste
- 8 tbsp breadcrumbs
- 8 ciabatta rolls, halved
- 8 tbsp tofu mayonnaise
- 8 leaves Romaine lettuce
- 1 medium tomato, sliced
- 1 onion, sliced

Preparation instructions
1. Insert crisper plates in both drawers. Spray the crisper plates with nonstick cooking oil.
2. Toss the aubergine rounds with olive oil, mustard, cumin, salt, black pepper, and breadcrumbs. Toss until they are well coated on all sides.
3. Select zone 1 and pair it with "AIR FRY" at 200°C for 15 minutes. Select "MATCH" followed by the "START/STOP" button.
4. Turn over aubergine rounds halfway through the cooking time to ensure even cooking.
5. Lastly, spread the rolls with tofu mayonnaise. Top the rolls with fried aubergine rounds, lettuce, tomato, and onion slices. Serve immediately and enjoy!

Roasted Winter Squash

Serves 5

Prep time: 10 minutes / Cook time: 25 minutes

Ingredients
- 1kg winter squash, cut into wedges
- 1 tsp coconut oil
- 1 tsp cayenne pepper
- Sea salt and ground black pepper, to taste
- 120g Kalamata olives, pitted and sliced
- 200g vegan coconut cream
- 10 cherry tomatoes, quartered

Preparation instructions
1. Insert crisper plates in both drawers. Spray the crisper plates with nonstick cooking oil.
2. Brush the winter squash with coconut oil, cayenne pepper, salt, and black pepper. Place the winter squash wedges in both drawers.
3. Select zone 1 and pair it with "ROAST" at 200°C for 25 minutes. Select "MATCH" followed by the "START/STOP" button.
4. Turn over winter squash wedges halfway through the cooking time to ensure even cooking.
5. Top the winter squash with olives, vegan cream, and cherry tomatoes.
6. Bon appétit!

Restaurant-Style Falafel

Serves 6

Prep time: 10 minutes / Cook time: 20 minutes

Ingredients

- 300g dried chickpeas, soaked overnight and drained
- 100g chickpea flour (besan)
- 1 tsp baking soda
- 2 tbsp tahini
- 2 garlic cloves, minced
- 1 onion, peeled and diced
- 1 medium bunch of parsley
- 1 tsp red pepper flakes
- Sea salt and freshly ground black pepper, to taste
- 1 tbsp olive oil

Preparation instructions

1. Insert crisper plates in both drawers. Spray the crisper plates with nonstick cooking oil.
2. Add the chickpeas, besan, baking soda, tahini, garlic, onion, parsley, red pepper, salt, black pepper, and olive oil to a bowl of your food processor (or high-speed blender). Process the Ingredients until everything is well incorporated.
3. Then, roll the mixture into equal balls using an ice cream scoop. Place the falafel in both drawers.
4. Select zone 1 and pair it with "AIR FRY" at 185°C for 20 minutes. Select "MATCH" followed by the "START/STOP" button.
5. Toss the drawers halfway through the cooking time to ensure even cooking.
6. Bon appétit!

Broccoli & Bean Croquettes

Serves 6

Prep time: 10 minutes / Cook time: 20 minutes

Ingredients

- 300g broccoli, grated
- 2 (400g) cans of white beans, rinsed drained and mashed
- 1 medium onion, finely chopped
- 2 small garlic cloves, minced
- 1 small bunch of coriander, chopped
- 100g breadcrumbs
- Sea salt and ground black pepper, to taste
- 1/2 tsp ground cumin
- 100ml vegan BBQ sauce
- 1 tbsp olive oil

Preparation instructions

1. Insert the crisper plates in both drawers and spray them with cooking oil.
2. In a mixing bowl, thoroughly combine all the Ingredients. Shape the mixture into equal balls and arrange them in the prepared drawers. Flatten the croquettes with the back of the fork.
3. Select zone 1 and pair it with "AIR FRY" at 180°C for 20 minutes. Select "MATCH" to duplicate settings across both zones. Press the "START/STOP" button.
4. When zone 1 time reaches 10 minutes, turn the balls over and spray them with cooking oil on the other side; reinsert the drawers to continue cooking.
5. Bon appétit!

Fried Tofu with Roasted Brussels Sprouts

Serves 5

Prep time: 5 minutes / Cook time: 20 minutes

Ingredients

- 500g firm tofu, pressed and cut into bite-sized cubes
- 4 tbsp vegan BBQ sauce
- 1 tsp red pepper flakes, crushed
- Sea salt and ground black pepper, to taste
- 2 tbsp corn flour
- 2 tbsp olive oil
- 1kg Brussels sprouts, cut into halves, stem removed
- 200g Swiss cheese, grated

Preparation instructions

1. Insert the crisper plates in both drawers and spray them with cooking oil.
2. Toss tofu cubes with BBQ sauce, red pepper, salt, black pepper, and corn flour. Brush tofu pieces with 1 tablespoon of olive oil and place them in the zone 1 drawer.
3. Toss Brussels sprouts with the remaining 1 tablespoon of olive oil, salt, and black pepper. Arrange Brussels sprouts in the zone 2 drawer.
4. Select zone 1 and pair it with "AIR FRY" at 200°C for 16 to 18 minutes. Select zone 2 and pair it with "ROAST" at 190°C for 20 minutes. Select "SYNC" followed by the "START/STOP" button.
5. When zone 1 time reaches 8 minutes, shake the drawer to ensure even cooking; reinsert the drawer to continue cooking.
6. When zone 2 time reaches 10 minutes, shake the drawer and top your Brussels sprouts with cheese; reinsert the drawer to continue cooking.
7. Bon appétit!

Vegan "Chicken" Nuggets

Serves 4

Prep time: 5 minutes / Cook time: 12 minutes

Ingredients

- 100g soy curls
- 100ml hot water
- 40g cornmeal
- 40g plain flour
- 1 tbsp nutritional yeast
- 1 tsp poultry seasoning mix
- 20ml plain non-dairy yoghurt

Preparation instructions

1. Insert the crisper plates in both drawers and spray them with cooking oil.
2. Soak soy curls in hot water for approximately 10 minutes. Drain the soy curls in a mesh sieve, squeezing out as much liquid as possible. (You can use the back of a spoon to press soy curls)
3. Combine cornmeal, flour, nutritional yeast, and poultry seasoning mix in a shallow bowl. Add the yoghurt to a large bowl.
4. Add soy curls to the bowl with yoghurt and gently stir to coat; then, roll soy curls over the dry flour mixture until they're all evenly coated. Arrange the prepared soy curls on crisper plates and spray them with cooking oil.
5. Select zone 1 and pair it with "AIR FRY" at 180°C for 12 minutes. Select "MATCH" to duplicate settings across both zones. Press the "START/STOP" button.

6. When zone 1 time reaches 6 minutes, turn the vegan nuggets over and spray them with cooking oil on the other side; reinsert the drawers to continue cooking.

7. Bon appétit!

Aubergine with Roasted Chickpeas

Serves 4

Prep time: 5 minutes / Cook time: 16 minutes

Ingredients

- 1 large aubergine, wide middle section cut into 8 rounds
- 2 tbsp mayonnaise
- 1/2 tsp ground cumin
- 1 tsp garlic granules
- Sea salt and ground black pepper, to taste
- 8 tbsp breadcrumbs
- 200g canned chickpeas, drained and rinsed
- 2 tbsp olive oil
- 1 tsp hot paprika
- Sea salt and ground black pepper, to taste

Preparation instructions

1. Insert the crisper plates in both drawers and spray them with cooking oil.

2. Toss aubergine with mayonnaise, cumin, garlic granules, salt, and black pepper. Press the aubergine rounds onto the breadcrumbs until they are well coated on all sides.

3. Brush aubergine rounds with 1 tablespoon of olive oil and arrange them in the zone 1 drawer.

4. Toss the drained and rinsed chickpeas with the remaining Ingredients and add them to the zone 2 drawer.

5. Select zone 1 and pair it with "AIR FRY" at

200°C for 15 minutes. Select zone 2 and pair it with "ROAST" at 190°C for 16 minutes. Select "SYNC" followed by the "START/ STOP" button.

6. When zone 1 time reaches 7 minutes, turn the aubergine rounds over to ensure even cooking; reinsert the drawer to continue cooking.

7. When zone 2 time reaches 10 minutes, shake the drawer and reinsert it to continue cooking.

8. Bon appétit!

Homemade Vegetarian Burgers

Serves 6

Prep time: 10 minutes / Cook time: 18 minutes

Ingredients

- 400g canned red kidney beans, drained and rinsed
- 400g quinoa, soaked overnight and rinsed
- 1 small celery root, peeled and grated
- 1 small carrot, trimmed and grated
- 1 small leek, finely chopped
- 2 garlic cloves, pressed
- 1 small egg, whisked
- 4 tbsp BBQ sauce
- Sea salt and ground black pepper, to taste
- 100g crushed crackers

Preparation instructions

1. Insert the crisper plates in both drawers and spray them with cooking oil.

2. In a mixing bowl, thoroughly combine all the Ingredients. Shape the mixture into 6 patties and lower them into both drawers.

3. Select zone 1 and pair it with "AIR FRY" at 180°C for 18 minutes. Select "MATCH" to duplicate settings across both zones. Press

the "START/STOP" button.

4. When zone 1 time reaches 9 minutes, turn the burgers over and reinsert the drawers to continue cooking.

5. Serve warm burgers with toppings of your choice and enjoy!

Teriyaki Vegetables

Serves 2

Prep time: 5 minutes / Cook time: 19 minutes

Ingredients

- 1 Small Broccoli
- 4 Mushrooms
- 1 Mixed Pepper
- 1 Medium Zucchini/Courgette
- 1 Tbsp Extra Virgin Olive Oil
- 2 Tsp Chinese Five Spice
- Salt & Pepper
- 3 Tbsp Healthy Teriyaki Sauce

Preparation instructions

1. Your vegetables should be cut up and diced before being added to a mixing bowl. Add salt, pepper, and Chinese five spice. oil of extra virgin olives in a bowl. Add to the ninja foodi air fryer basket after thoroughly mixing.

2. 14 minutes of air frying at 180°C.

3. With your hands, remove the vegetables from the bowl and add them back in. Next, add the teriyaki sauce, mix well, and then transfer to a sheet of foil. Rearrange in the air fryer and cook for an additional 5 minutes at 180°C

Homemade Vegan Burgers

Serves 6

Prep time: 10 minutes / Cook time: 20 minutes

Ingredients

- 2 tbsp soy flakes
- 300g buckwheat, soaked overnight and rinsed
- 1 (400g) can of red lentils, rinsed and drained
- 1 small bunch of parleys
- 2 spring onions
- 100g breadcrumbs
- Sea salt and ground black pepper, to taste
- 1 tbsp smoked paprika
- 1 tsp mustard seeds
- 100g tub salsa

Preparation instructions

1. Insert the crisper plates in both drawers and spray them with cooking oil.

2. Soak soy flakes in 4 tbsp of hot water for about 10 minutes.

3. In your blender or a food processor, thoroughly combine all the Ingredients. Shape the mixture into 6 to 8 equal burger patties and arrange them in both drawers Brush each burger patty with cooking oil.

4. Select zone 1 and pair it with "AIR FRY" at 185°C for 20 minutes. Select "MATCH" to duplicate settings across both zones. Press the "START/STOP" button.

5. When zone 1 time reaches 10 minutes, carefully turn the burger patties over using a wide spatula. After that, spray them with cooking oil on the other side, and reinsert the drawers to continue cooking.

6. Serve warm patties with toppings of your choice.

7. Bon appétit!

Granola Bars

Serves 6

Prep time: 10 minutes / Cook time: 20 minutes

Ingredients

- 100g oats
- 50g coconut oil (or butter), melted
- 50g raw pumpkin seeds, chopped
- 20g sesame seeds
- 50g almonds, chopped
- 100g honey
- 6-8 prunes, pitted and chopped
- 1 tsp vanilla essence
- 1/2 tsp grated nutmeg
- 1 tsp ground cinnamon
- 1/2 tsp ground cloves

Preparation instructions

1. In a mixing bowl, thoroughly combine all the Ingredients. Line two roasting tins with baking paper.
2. Tip the granola mixture into the prepared tins, pressing down lightly. Add roasting tins to both drawers (without crisper plates).
3. Select zone 1 and pair it with "BAKE" at 180°C for 20 minutes. Select "MATCH" to duplicate settings across both zones. Press the "START/STOP" button.
4. Let it cool on a wire rack and then, cut it into bars. Enjoy!

Street-Style Corn on the Cob

Serves 6

Prep time: 10 minutes / Cook time: 19 minutes

Ingredients

- 4 ears corn on the cob, halved
- 60g butter, room temperature
- 60g cream cheese, room temperature
- 1 garlic clove, crushed
- 1 tsp red pepper flakes, crushed
- 1 tbsp fresh parsley leaves, minced

Preparation instructions

1. Insert the crisper plates in both drawers and spray them with cooking oil. Cut four pieces of foil large enough to hold a cob.
2. Lower a cob on each piece of foil, and top them with butter; lastly, seal the edges to form parcels. Place them in both drawers.
3. Select zone 1 and pair it with "AIR FRY" at 190°C for 18 to 19 minutes. Select "MATCH" to duplicate settings across both zones. Press the "START/STOP" button.
4. Garnish corn on the cob with cream cheese, garlic, red pepper, and parsley.
5. Bon appétit!

Roasted Vegetables with Tofu

Serves 5

Prep time: 10 minutes / Cook time: 20 minutes

Ingredients

- 1 large aubergine, cut into rounds
- 2 large carrots, cut into long sticks
- 1 medium courgette, cut into rounds
- 2 bell peppers, seeded and halved
- 1 large onion, sliced
- 200g tofu, pressed and cubed
- 2 tbsp soy sauce
- 1 tbsp Dijon mustard
- 1 tbsp olive oil
- 1 tsp garlic granules
- 1 red pepper flakes
- Sea salt and ground black pepper, to taste
-

Preparation instructions

1. Toss your vegetables and tofu with the other Ingredients. Divide aubergine rounds, carrots, and courgettes between two lightly greased baking tins.
2. Lower the baking tins into both drawers (without a crisper plate inserted).
3. Select zone 1 and pair it with "ROAST" at 190°C for 20 minutes. Select "MATCH" to duplicate settings across both zones. Press the "START/STOP" button.
4. After that, add the peppers, onion, and tofu to the baking tins; reinsert the drawers to continue cooking.
5. Taste and adjust the seasoning. Bon appétit!

Harvest Casserole

Serves 2

Prep time: 5minutes / Cook time: 20 minutes

Ingredients

- 100 g Fresh Sprouts
- 2 Red Apples
- 2 Green Apples
- 4 Sausages
- 3 Slices Thick Bacon chopped into bits
- 1 Medium Sweet Potato
- ½ Medium White Onion
- 1 Tbsp Extra Virgin Olive Oil
- 2 Tbsp Thyme
- Salt & Pepper

Preparation instructions

1. Apples should be peeled and cut into cubes. Your sweet potato should be peeled and cut into cubes, as well as your onion. Your sprouts should be cleaned and quartered.
2. Add thyme, extra virgin olive oil, salt, and pepper to a bowl. Use your hands to

combine the spice and oil until you have a decent coating.
3. Place the food inside the Ninja foodi air fryer and cook for 8 minutes at 180 °C (360 °F).
4. Slice your sausages into medium-sized pieces and chop your bacon into bacon bits while the air fryer is working its magic. Shake the basket and place the sausage and bacon on top when the air fryer sounds. Cook at the same temperature for ten minutes.
5. Shake the air fryer and combine the fruit and vegetables with the sausage and bacon. Before serving, cook for an additional 2 minutes at 200°C/400 f.
6. Alternately, increase the cook time by 7 minutes rather of 2, and spritz with extra virgin olive oil for crispier results.

Grilled Aubergine Rolls with Tofu

Serves 5

Prep time: 10 minutes / Cook time: 17 minutes

Ingredients

- 2 medium aubergines, slice lengthways into 1/2cm-thick slices
- 2 bell peppers, deveined and cut into halves
- Sea salt and ground black pepper, to taste
- 1 tsp paprika
- 1 tsp garlic granules
- 1/2 tsp ground cumin
- 1 tbsp olive oil
- 200g tofu, pressed and chopped
- 4 sun-dried tomatoes in oil, chopped

Preparation instructions

1. Insert the crisper plates in both drawers and spray them with cooking oil.

2. Toss aubergine slices and bell peppers with spices and olive oil. Arrange them in both drawers.

3. Select zone 1 and pair it with "ROAST" at 190°C for 12 minutes. Select "MATCH" to duplicate settings across both zones. Press the "START/STOP" button.

4. Meanwhile, mix crumbled tofu with sun-dried tomatoes and reserve. Add chopped roasted peppers to the mixture.

5. Top the aubergine slices with the tofu mixture; roll them up and secure them with toothpicks; carefully lower the aubergine rolls into both drawers.

6. Select zone 1 and pair it with "AIR FRY" at 180°C for 5 minutes. Select "MATCH" to duplicate settings across both zones. Press the "START/STOP" button.

7. Bon appétit!

Buffalo Cauliflower Wings

Serves 5

Prep time: 10 minutes / Cook time: 20 minutes

Ingredients
- 1kg cauliflower florets
- 1 tbsp olive oil
- 2 tbsp vegan Worcestershire sauce
- 1 tsp ground cumin
- 1 tsp garlic granules
- 1 tsp hot paprika
- Sea salt and ground black pepper, to taste

Preparation instructions
1. Insert the crisper plates in both drawers and spray them with cooking oil.

2. Place the cauliflower florets, along with the other Ingredients, in a resealable bag; give it a good shake until the cauliflower florets are well coated on all sides.

3. Select zone 1 and pair it with "ROAST" at 200°C for 20 minutes. Select "MATCH" to duplicate settings across both zones. Press the "START/STOP" button.

4. After 10 minutes, toss the drawers and reinsert them to continue cooking.

5. Bon appétit!

Fried Avocado Tacos

Serves 4

Prep time: 30 minutes / Cook time: 10 minutes

Ingredients
- 170 g shredded fresh kale or coleslaw mix
- 21 g minced fresh cilantro
- 85 g cup plain Greek yogurt
- 2 tablespoons lime juice
- 1 teaspoon honey
- 1/4 teaspoon salt
- 1/4 teaspoon ground chipotle pepper
- 1/4 teaspoon pepper

TACOS Ingredients
- 1 large egg, beaten
- 32 g cornmeal
- 1/2 teaspoon salt
- 1/2 teaspoon garlic powder
- 1/2 teaspoon ground chipotle pepper
- 2 medium avocados, peeled and sliced
- Cooking spray
- 8 flour tortillas or corn tortillas (6 inches)
- 1 medium tomato, chopped
- Crumbled queso fresco, optional

Preparation instructions
1. In a bowl, mix the first 8 Ingredients. Keep chilled until serving, covered.

2. Set the air fryer to 400 degrees. Egg should

be put in a small bowl. Combine cornmeal, salt, garlic powder, and chipotle pepper in a separate shallow basin. Avocado slices should be dipped in egg, then lightly patted into a cornmeal mixture to help them adhere.

3. Avocado slices should be placed in single layers on a greased tray in the Ninja Foodi air fryer basket and sprayed with cooking spray as you go. Cook for 4 minutes or until golden brown. Toss with cooking spray and turn. Cook for 3–4 more minutes, or until golden brown.

4. Avocado slices should be served in tortillas along with kale mixture, tomato, more chopped cilantro, and, if preferred, queso fresco.

Vegan Wraps

Serves 4

Prep time: 10 minutes / Cook time: 10 minutes

Ingredients

- 500g mushrooms, wiped and cut into quarters
- 1 tsp garlic granules
- 1 tsp paprika
- 120g tortilla chips, crushed
- 2 tbsp olive oil
- 400g tempeh, pressed and sliced
- 2 tbsp tomato ketchup
- 2 tbsp vegan mayonnaise
- 1 tsp mustard
- 5 tortilla wraps, warmed

Preparation instructions

1. Insert the crisper plates in both drawers and spray them with cooking oil.

2. In a mixing bowl, thoroughly combine the mushrooms with spices, crushed tortilla chips, and 1 teaspoon of olive oil. Arrange your mushrooms in the zone 1 drawer.

3. Brush tempeh with ketchup and the remaining 1 tablespoon of olive oil; place the tempeh slices in the zone 2 drawer.

4. Select zone 1 and pair it with "AIR FRY" at 200°C for 7 minutes. Select zone 2 and pair it with "AIR FRY" at 180°C for 10 minutes. Select "SYNC" followed by the "START/STOP" button.

5. When zone 1 time reaches 3 minutes, toss the drawer to ensure even cooking; reinsert the drawer to continue cooking.

6. When zone 2 time reaches 5 minutes, shake the drawer and reinsert it to continue cooking.

7. Assemble vegan wraps with tortilla wraps, air-fried mushrooms, tempeh, mayonnaise, and mustard.

8. Bon appétit!

Printed in Great Britain
by Amazon